Making a P O E M

SOME THOUGHTS
ABOUT POETRY
AND THE PEOPLE
WHO WRITE IT

D1202781

LOUISIANA STATE UNIVERSITY PRESS)|(BATON ROUGE

Published by Louisiana State University Press
Copyright © 2006 by Louisiana State University Press
All rights reserved
Manufactured in the United States of America

An LSU Press Paperback Original
First printing

Designer: Laura Roubique Gleason
Typefaces: Minion text, Universe display
Printer and binder: Edwards Brothers, Inc.

LIBRARY OF CONGRESS CATALOGING-IN-PUBLICATION DATA
Williams, Miller.
  Making a poem : some thoughts about poetry and the people who write it /
Miller Williams.
      p.   cm.
ISBN-13 978-0-8071-3132-9 (pbk.)
ISBN-10 0-8071-3132-6 (pbk. : alk. paper)
1. American poetry—History and criticism—Theory, etc.   2. Poetry—
Authorship.   3. Poetics.   4. Authors and publishers.   I. Title.
PS303.W44 2006
811.009—dc22

                                                2006001333

The paper in this book meets the guidelines for permanence and durability of
the Committee on Production Guidelines for Book Longevity of the Council
on Library Resources. ♾

The following essays have been published previously: "Intuition, Spontaneity,
Organic Wholeness, and the Redemptive Wilderness" in *The Smith* (April
1976); "A Case for Rhyme and Meter" in *Writer's Digest* (July 1996); "Translate"
in the *Barataria Review* (1975); "Let Me Not to the Marriage of True Minds" in
Evidence (1967); "The Writer and the Editor" in *Scholarly Publishing* (February
1983); and "What Stone Walls Make" in *Books* (March 1974).

Making a POEM

Miller Williams

Deep thanks to John and Jordan, co-authors both

CONTENTS

Poetry and Poetics

Nobody Plays the Piano, but We Like to Have It in the House

$\mathcal{W}$e live in a haunted world. We are surrounded by ghosts. Reminders of past and nearly forgotten days are all about us, things neither alive nor dead from an old world. We see them, but we may not notice. We may not recognize them as ghosts, relics of a nearly forgotten past. The buttons on a man's coat sleeve, which once held his lace cuff out of his soup; the touching of glasses in a toast, which is what we have left from the days when two royal friends would mix a bit of their drinks together to assure each other that no poisoning was going on; the shaking of hands, which was once a way of showing a person we met that we carried no weapon.

These are souvenirs now, parts of the past that have stayed to haunt our culture. In general, because we are nostalgic creatures, we like having them with us, and there's nothing wrong with that. We'd be poorer without them.

Some things, though, have been relegated to the china cabinet and the mantelpiece that maybe should not be there, things that are still important to us, or ought to be important to us, though we keep them only as souvenirs, to show only where we came from, that we are not barbarians, as we may keep the coat of arms framed on the wall, the copy of *War and Peace* on the end table, the French cookbook in the kitchen. I know a wealthy family with a priceless concert grand in their living room. It's been there for at least three generations. For at least two generations no one in the family has been able to play it. The piano serves no more purpose than to show not who these people are but who they believe they were. We give some room and some attention to our noblest relics because they give us, in return, prestige and self-satisfaction. They help us to persuade ourselves that we are seekers not of the coin and the crown but of the scholar's gown and the wreath of laurel and some perhaps not unholy grail. We know who we should be. We want to look as if, to sound as if, that's who we are. So to that collection of things we keep because we are too nostalgic to let them go—the touching of glasses and the tipping of hats and the awkward sword of the military cadet—we add a collection of things we keep because we are ashamed to let them go even though we are not sure we have a place for them in this world.

So we keep the big book on the end table, the piano in the living room, a high-school class in French, and perhaps a class in poetry. With the true relics our desire has outlived our need. But with the poetry nobody knows how to read as with the piano nobody knows how to play, our need has outlived our desire.

I suggest that we either trade the piano in for a laser CD deck or learn to play it. I ask your indulgence in allowing me to speak for the second of these options so that we might more effectively come to poetry while we are in school and understand the uses of poetry in the world outside the academy. If I argue that we have generally failed in this so far, I do not mean it to be a universal indictment. We are apparently raising some young people who are not left entirely cold by poetry.

I know this because recently I came across the work of such a student as I was eating breakfast in the snack shop on a college campus. I found the words of a young scholar who had learned to respond to literature with feeling. The words were carved deep into the table in bold, block letters: "Tennyson was a nerd and Browning was a male chauvinist pig."

Let's say that a lot of us have not learned to respond to poetry with even that kind of conviction. Let's admit that to many of us poetry is a decoration, a sign of class and good grace that has little to do with our lives. Even some of us to whom poetry is important allow it the importance of ornamentation and hesitate to say that it matters as much as golf or tennis or that it has the substance of, say, painting. Painting, we say, is "real" art. Museums are built for it; money is paid for it. People steal it.

Let's consider for a while what poetry is and what it does and why it ought to matter to us once the final school bell rings— and why too often it does not.

Let me begin by suggesting some things I think we are often doing wrong, in our homes and in our classrooms.

We begin to dwarf the natural poetic impulse of children— if there is one, and I'm inclined to believe that there is—before they ever get into school, as when a child runs into the house saying, "Hey, there's a lion in the yard!" and we say, "Don't be silly, that's a dog. You know the difference between a dog and a lion." The child has just done what a poem does. To the child, the thing in the yard was not a dog. It *was* a lion, because looking at it the child felt "lion" not "dog." The child senses that the dimensions of a thing are not the essence of a thing, that what something does to us is part of its essential nature, and so a child describes a thing in terms of its effects. So does a poem. The poet and the child are interested not in how many feet there are to a mile but in how many steps there are.

The poet in the child is crippled, I think, when the child is conditioned to expect an answer whenever there is a question.

It comes to me sometimes that the real problem students have in coming to poetry is this: they are unable to accept something that deliberately raises questions it doesn't answer or for which there is no answer.

We sometimes seem to want poetry to be a branch of philosophy or religion. It may be the business of religion, and the business of philosophy, to answer questions, and if it is, I can't blame them for being about their business. But I can insist that we should not damn poetry for being something other than religion or philosophy and that it makes more sense to call poetry philosophy than it does to call philosophy poetry.

But we're not through. Once we get the child, the boy especially, into school, we go to work in earnest. We forget—those of us who were boys and have known—what it means to be between boyhood and manhood, with too much beard to ignore and too little to shave and three or four voices interrupting one another. As if it weren't bad enough that we're ungainly and often pimply, the girls we know when we are entering our awkward age are just leaving theirs. We never looked less like men, and we feel this doubly because they never looked so much like women. We're determined to prove the young manhood we feel uneasy about, and so we boast and fight our parents and teachers, and we use bad language and live in two-fisted fantasies. We're looking everywhere for anything that will make us feel virile, heroic, raunchy. So we go into the classroom and are told to stand and read something about "my heart leaps up when I behold daffodils and rainbows and birds thou never wert."

And then we have the student lift the "story" from the poem in paraphrase without ever telling the student that what is left behind is poetry.

This is not to say that a poem ought to be without meaning.

There is no communication of being; it is meaning we communicate. A poem has to mean, but a good poet knows, and a good reader knows, that some things cannot be said directly, will not be looked at straight, are seen only out of the corner of the eye. You may have noticed, as you looked at the sky or a distant landscape, the ghost twig that sometimes floats barely into your field of vision. You're aware of it. You can tell its shape and almost its color. You can see it move. But when you turn your eye to focus more clearly on it, it leaps away. You can't look at it when you try to; you can see it only when you are looking at something else. A great deal of the experience of poetry lies in this indirection. When we turn our eyes to the denotation of the poem, it has a way of slipping from our field of vision, but we come by the experience of the poem, not by paraphrase, to an insight, an awareness about people that we didn't have before.

Experience always leads the open mind to insight, something more valuable than the comprehension we are led to by logic. It seems to me that Cardinal Newman's distinction between Notional Assent and Real Assent has meaning here. He saw Notional Assent as the agreement one gives by intelligence to some statement, some thesis or proposition. Real Assent is the agreement that comes from experience, from having been there, so that we know more surely than reason could tell us that, say, "War is hell" or "Love makes the world go 'round." Now let's say, for example, that a young woman is sitting on her front porch rocking and thinking about Plato's Scale of Being or the Categorical Imperative when a mail carrier comes up and says, "Love makes the world go 'round." She says, "Well, that sounds alright. I mean, love gets us married, and marriage gets us kids, and kids get us perpetuated. So, okay. It makes sense. Love makes the world go 'round in a metaphorical way." She has considered the proposition and given it Notional Assent. Then let's say that a few weeks later the summer is over, she's gone back to school for the fall term, and she's just bought all her books in the campus bookstore. She's heading back to her room with the books piled higher than her head when she bumps into another student and the books fall to the floor. She sees even as she starts to kick him in the shins that he is beautiful. He bends down to help her pick up the books, and she bends down to help him, and they bump heads. It's a 1940s movie. They both look up to apologize and their eyes meet, and that's it. Wow! Pow! All that.

Then three or four days later a police officer stops her and says, "Love makes the world go 'round," and she says, "Yeah!" Because, you see, she's been there. She's had the experience. This is not Notional Assent anymore. This is Real Assent.

There is also what must be called Real Assent—compared, certainly, with what we learn from argument and observation—in our response to the love poems of John Donne. And compared with what we learn from the newspapers or casualty lists, or even from television, there is Real Assent to the proposition that "War is hell" after a reading of Wilfred Owen's "Dulce et Decorum Est" because here too we are involved, we are drawn in. We participate. We experience the poem, and through that experience we come to insight.

The experience that brings us to this insight is the end of the poem, the end of the rhyme, irony, indirection, metaphor, image, and all the devices of language that a poet learns to use to make a poem.

What we have to ask of the poem is that it work, that it offer us an experience that we can believe is a part of our world. That it be, in a word, honest.

Now to say that a poem is dishonest is the same as saying it's a bad poem. I have difficulty, though, thinking in terms of bad poetry. I prefer to call it phony poetry because in a manner of speaking there is no such thing as a bad poem.

When I was a boy, I think, all Methodist preachers, at least those in the hills and the small towns, had had their throats burned out by God himself with a terrible poker that reached from heaven for the purpose, and the throats had been filled with hot coals that rumbled against one another when the preacher spoke, giving off the smell of something on fire.

I remember listening with my whole body as a young prophet described Armageddon: it was to be the battle to the death between the good angels and the bad angels. I think this is where my first doubt began. I knew that whatever a preacher could do with words, there was no such thing as a bad angel, that one was a good angel or one was simply not an angel at all. The definition of goodness was implicit in the word *angel*—and the definitions of quality, of rightness, of efficacy, I like to believe, are implicit in the word *art* and in the word *poem.*

This may seem to be semantic tail-chasing, but I don't believe it is. I think it's important what we teach our children and ourselves to call poetry and I believe it makes a great difference whether we call a rose by another name.

More, it's important to know that we do not come to Milton and Auden and Bishop through the "oh, God, the beauty" poets on one hand or the "let me show you my mucous" poets on the other. A good poem has more in common with good painting than it does with a counterfeit poem.

What is the difference between the real and the counterfeit in poetry? What gives away a thing that looks like a poem but isn't?

That is, why do we not respond to it? This is, after all, the thing about a poem. It must have the power to make us respond, to make us more alive. We have to react to it, taking part even in its creation.

If I were to make a list of the signs of a counterfeit poem, a warning to go on the front of a cash register in some land where poems are currency, the list would run about like this:

The first giveaway might be some kind of sentimentalism. Now, there are varieties of sentimentalism in poetry, the most common being the attempt to give superficial thought, shallow ideas, the shape of importance; the attempt to give ephemeral things the shape of profundity—crying out to heaven over the loss of a ballgame or the failure to get an invitation to a party.

Another is the use of what I call "instant emotion," the use of terms to which we have been so conditioned that it's no longer necessary to say something with the words. It's enough simply to use them. Tear-stained Bible, the Transylvanian Way of Life, Tattered Flag, Dear Old Dad, Somebody's Mother, the old homeplace, Manifest Destiny.

This is the sort of sentimentality that the writers of protest poems and polemics on both the right and the left almost always fall into, a kind of push-button feeling that may be easy to evoke in one who understands the world through bumper stickers, but when we respond to the words only, we are responding to air.

Then a thing may fail as a poem because it tries to do what a poem cannot do: it tries to become a treatise on cosmic truth. This is most often because the writer has tried to pin down what won't be still. Getting back to the value of indirection, we can best be exact about the cosmic things—God and truth, beauty, eternity, and love—by not talking directly about them. In a metaphor we see a thing by reflection off another surface, which is not only an interesting way to look at something but necessary when we are dealing with a thing that can't be caught head-on. We see the wind in the grass because the wind is invisible. We see the sun in the lake because the sun is too bright. We have to see the face of whatever truth there is reflected off the surface of a shield. Our reflecting shield is the metaphor.

And there is more to this. We *want* to see less than all there is because this is the only way in which our imaginations can be called to participate in making the poem whole. Because a poem does not exist on the page. It exists when the imagination of the writer and the imagination of the reader confront each other in an act of language to make that act complete. John Aubrey, the seventeenth-century man about town and letters, reminds us of this in his journals: "As Pythagoras did guess at the vastness of Hercules' stature by the length of his foot, so we are there pleased most where something keeps the eye from being lost and leaves us room to guess."

We want to scrounge around in the poem, to take part in its perfection. Something that involves only the expected, we cannot respond to, we cannot even stay awake with.

If we want to put a person to sleep, we can do it by simply removing from the environment—from notice, that is—any change that is not expected. Put a person in a rocking chair so that the movement of the rocker conceals any smaller motion, while each new sweep of the rocker is anticipated and therefore ignored, or turn on an air conditioner so that the hum of the motor drowns out smaller sounds, while each wave of sound from the motor is anticipated and therefore ignored, and you will see that the mind, experiencing then a kind of constancy of the anticipated—may I offer that as a fair definition of monotony?—experiencing a constancy of the anticipated, goes to rest, goes to sleep.

And then the *deformed metaphor* is found in a lot of what only looks like poetry. The metaphor fully conceived and cleanly wrought does more perhaps than anything else to take us inside the poem. We see in a good metaphor and in a simile the images they create by their nature, an implied unity—a kinship—between things whose common parts we might not have suspected. The implication is intriguing, and we are drawn into the line to confirm the kinship for ourselves, to confirm it by an act of intellect and of imagination. To make it real, to realize it. From Dylan Thomas:

> And I must enter again the round
> Zion of the water bead
> and the synagogue of the ear of corn

And from T. S. Eliot:

> Let us go then, you and I,
> When the evening is spread out against the sky
> Like a patient etherized upon a table;

From Wallace Stevens:

> Out of the window,
> I saw how the planets gathered
> Like the leaves themselves
> Turning in the wind.

The image, or submerged metaphor, that we find in sort-of-poetry may, as I say, be deformed. Witness these little grotesques. The first is from a high-school anthology. Try to see this, as one will always try to see a metaphor, on the literal level first. It's about what heaven will be like:

I will gather grapes in the bosom of Abraham. . . .

This was in a poemlike thing submitted for publication in the *New Orleans Review* when I was its editor.

> My heart stands on tiptoe to kiss
> the pinnacle of your soul. . . .

I don't know what they're doing there, but I think that even in New Orleans you get arrested for it. And this was also in a submission to the *Review:*

> Come build a fire with me
> in the lap of Venus,
> and let no land or ocean
> come between us.

And this:

> The night comes in like the tide
> and whispers in my ear
> and I rest in its dark and leafy arms
> where there is no fear.

I was impressed. Most people would have been terrified.

We don't have to look to amateurs, though, for this sort of thing. Stephen Spender, a fine poet who certainly knew better, spoke of a bee as "one cog in a golden hive."

I have said a lot about response, but I don't know any other terms in which one can talk about poetry. To respond is to be alive; to cease to respond is to cease to be alive. The stone and the frog are most importantly different in this: When there is a change in the environment of the frog, the frog changes against that change in such a way as will tend to minimize it, to negate it, and in order to maintain within the frog a kind of constant state. The rock changes passively with the change around it.

The change in the frog, the change in us—the reaction against the direction of change in our environment—creates tension. It's this tension that is life, to the body and to the mind.

I'm not offering a cure for the world's ills, or pep pills for the despondent, or a way to happiness, but I am committed to the belief that poetry—as well as painting and sculpture, music and dance and drama—in a time when we are sometimes tempted to pull away from the world, in a time when there is so much to withdraw from, in a time when we may forget that to be a little bit numb, to be a little anesthetized, is to be a little bit dead, may in a small way help to keep us alive.

And richly alive, if we invest something of ourselves in the act of language in which the poet has already made at least half the investment.

Because a poem reminds us to see, not things, but one thing and one thing and one thing, as a poem is built of images.

And a poem reminds us to see the relations between things, as a poem is built of metaphor.

And a poem reminds us of the good meaning of order, as a poem is built of language moving through a pattern.

But there is more to poetry than this.

We come, or might come by poems, to understand the ironic vision, that abiding realization that most human statements contain their own contradictions and that most human acts contain the seeds of their own defeat.

It has been reported by the *New York Times,* for instance, that as technology increases, more and more people are coming to believe in an active and personal devil. The scientists and educators interviewed were astounded and confused. No one who reads and responds to poetry could be either astounded or confused.

And then a poem might remind us of compassion, as a poet refuses to populate poems with people who are simply good or simply bad. As a poet has to know and has to tell us that everyone we meet is a battlefield.

And then a poem might remind us of the difference between just stopping and coming to a close, which is one of the frequent differences between life and art.

And then a poem might remind us that we can afford to give up everything but beginnings.

And then a poem might bring us to an expanded sense of the game ritual by which all of us give meaning to our lives when we are not simply surviving. John Ciardi defined *game,* which includes poetry and basketball and chess and crossword puzzles, as a human activity made difficult for the joy of it. I don't suggest that poetry ought to be covered in *Sports Illustrated,* but I do suggest that it ought not be any more foreign to our world than that, and that it might make our lives, for all of our lives, more meaningful.

Well, I still hear someone say, "I don't know, I just don't understand it, I don't have the ear for it." And I say to that in one of my rare literary allusions, "Bah! Humbug!" There are little pieces of poetry all around us, and we do respond to them; things, that is, which we understand with the same part of us that understands poetry. Let me offer some examples, and let me say that one who understands what is remarkable and ambiguous in them is using at least one part of the mind that understands poetry.

I have a friend who has been teaching English for forty-three years, and for all of them he has drawn strength from a misspelling that appeared in the first group of themes he ever assigned: "Life is so short," it said, "that we must make the most of every minuet."

Recently I was approached by a casual acquaintance, a young nun, who said, "Excuse me, Mr. Williams, but if you don't mind my asking, what is your faith?" Now, I've never been able to find the right name for what I believe, so to be as honest as I could in a few words I said, "Well, I suppose you'd call me a Druid." "Oh," she said, with ecumenical tolerance. "And is that Protestant?"

In the rolling credits after a movie about Moses I read this disturbing line: "The voice of the burning bush was prerecorded."

A loan company in New Orleans recently announced across the glass of its window: "Now you can borrow enough money to get completely out of debt."

In the registration line at the University of Arkansas recently I heard a young woman ask, "Does anyone know who's taking care of Western Civilization?"

I was watching television, alone in the house, one past Easter season when my teeth were rattled and the world jarred to life by this line from a commercial in the deep and mellifluous tones of a man's voice: "Eat at Bob and Jake's this week; enjoy Lent more than ever."

I was looking for something to read—anything to read—on a commuter flight a few months ago when I found this lovely moment of accidental wisdom on a sick bag: "To ease discomfort, concentrate on some distant object."

These are fragments. They are, of course, not art. They are not poems. But they have about them something of what is important in a poem. They say much more than the statement they make; these meanings that come rising up to us from under the surface have an insistent truth about them, and when we try to focus on it, to look hard at it, it's gone.

What I'm saying is that poetry—the impulse to make it and the power to understand it—is not something exotic, something foreign to our minds. It is, or it ought to be, part of our lives from the time we shake our cribs in rhythm and wake our parents yelling "*bah* bah *bah* bah *bah*" until we come through "Little Jack Horner" and "Hey Diddle Diddle" to Emily Dickinson and William Butler Yeats. Some, of course, get sidetracked and never complete their development. They tell you that poetry is for kids and old folks, that it's for schoolteachers, that it's silly stuff and doesn't make sense—and then they go off to a football game and stand up, flag in one hand and beer in the other, yelling,

> Bo Bo Skee-watn-datn,
> I beneetn-doe!
> Skiddy-bee, skiddy-bo,
> Hey, team, let's go!

We need poetry as we need love and company. It's a matter, finally, of whether we bring into our lives the real thing, naked and demanding, or something we simply inflate to look like the real thing, which neither demands nor gives.

Some Observations on the Line in Poetry

To pay attention to the line is not to suggest that a poem exists on the page. It doesn't. A poem comes into existence when the imagination of a writer and the imagination of a reader confront each other inside an act of language. The writer and the reader bring to that confrontation different imaginations structured by different associations. The poem in print is the ground on which the meeting takes place.

The line is the structural and functional unit of the printed poem, as decidedly as the paragraph is the unit of both structure and function in exposition, and as the scene is in fiction.

This is not to say that the line is necessarily a unit of sense, of course, but that a poem doesn't work as a poem when the lines don't work as lines. The question is, what does it mean for a line to work? The answer is, to borrow a phrase of Auden's, simple and hard. It means that at the end of a line the reader feels rhythmically pleased but expectant. It is this expectation that creates much of a good poem's sense of forward motion, and, in the fulfillment of this expectation, the sense of pleasure. In the case of the last line the expectation will be for nothing to follow, which is the most radical change in the poem.

The anticipation created by the line's ending, except in that last line, may be for the completion of a rhythmical pattern: "Shave and a haircut / six bits."

It may be for the completion of a statement, which is to say, simply, that the line is enjambed; that is, the statement is not completed until the next line.

In verse with a pattern of rhyme the expectation is partly for the completion of the pattern each time a rhyme is begun. To speak of a pattern of rhyme is still to speak of the line because rhyme (assuming that it's terminal) is a form of line break and thus is a function of the line.

Frequently, especially in freer verse, where there is no dependable pattern of rhyme and therefore no expectation, the end of a line will raise a question in the reader's mind, and the beginning of the next line will provide an answer. Here are some examples of how the reader is involved in this kind of juncture. From Louis Simpson's "American Poetry":

> Whatever it is, it must have
> A stomach that can digest
> Rubber, coal, uranium, moons, poems.

From Archibald MacLeish's "Winter Is Another Country":

> if this would end
> I could endure the absence in the night
> The hands beyond the reach of time, the name
> Called out. . . .

And also in more formal verse, from William Meredith's "The Open Sea":

> Nor does it signify, that people who stay
> Very long, bereaved or not, at the edge of the sea
> Hear the drowned folk call. . . .

At the line breaks in these brief passages a reader can ask—a good reader will ask—"What?" or "Then what?" or "How long?" The asking and the move to the answer not only propel the reader through the poem but heighten the reader's sense of participation in the poem.

Every time a word is added to a poem, the poet has made a decision about a line's relative and absolute length; every time a line is ended with a rhyme word, the poet has made a decision about the quality of sound setting up a rhyme set or decides whether to answer the first sound with true or slant rhyme. In the case of topographical or spatial poems, like many of Cummings's and Ferlinghetti's, a decision is made about the placement of the line on the page. It's by means of all this that a poet makes the line, and the poem, a more effective construction so that it becomes a more convincing illusion of conversation.

If a reader is to take part in the experience of a poem, the poem must be credibly of this world. We trust minds that talk our talk, and we're excited by minds that talk it with energy and that leave as much as possible still to be said; minds, that is, that invite us into dialogue in our own language about the phenomenological world we live in. What is not always recognized is the intriguing relationship between reality and illusion.

Plain talk doesn't make for conversationality in poetry. The very fact of a poem is theatrical, and we know that the realm of Prufrock is not the "real" world but an illusion of the world, or a part of it, as the stage is in a theater.

Reality in a framework of illusion (an actual living-room conversation in a play) or illusion in a context of reality (Lear's mad scene at a bus stop) gives a sense of the grotesque. Reality in a context of the "actual," phenomenological world or illusion in a context of a posited world gives a sense of the real.

This obviously invites a discussion of diction, but it's something that wants saying—I think it insists on being said—in an examination of any aspect of poetry, and it bears directly, as I mean to show, on the study of the line. We engineer the line and contrive line breaks so that the reader, in a context of illusion not unlike that represented by the proscenium arch, believes that the lines are natural things for a human to utter; decides to believe it, that is, wants to and does, as we believe Hamlet when he's on the stage but not when he's on the sidewalk.

Poetry, like all art, is ritual, and ritual doesn't want conversation. The poet balances the two demands, plays conversationality against form, and finds in this tension much of the energy that means life to a poem. Some of the most effective means of holding this balance, of heightening the sense of ritual or increasing the sense of spontaneity, are discovered in the way the lines end. Enjambment tends to increase the feeling of conversation; end stopping (punctuation at the ends of lines) tends to increase the feeling that the reader is involved in a ritual act. Enjambment increases the sense of the lyric and compromises the ritualistic effect of rhyme.

Enjambment was especially popular with the Elizabethan poets but, understandably, was not much favored by the neoclassicists. The romantic poets returned to the practice as an important aspect of their release from the formal strictures of the poetry of their recent past. The French, German, and Spanish histories are not very different. Attitudes toward enjambment, from disapproval to tolerance to preference, have changed as the larger critical and aesthetic views of the society's literature have shifted. Slant rhyme, still dealing with rhyme as a form of line break, makes a poem more conversational than true rhyme, less conversational than no rhyme.

The metrics of the line break requires us to make finer distinctions, but before turning to them I feel compelled to deal with a general misapprehension concerning metrics: the nature of the foot at the end of a line is as relevant to nonpatterned poetry as it is to what we call formal poetry. No matter how purely accentual a line may be until the end, it's in the nature of the language that the last syllables in the line are going to be recognizable and that we're going to hear them as accented or not. This is the same thing as saying that we're going to recognize the terminal foot. The poet has to take this into account or lose some control over what the poem is doing.

The iambic or anapestic ending conveys a greater sense of formality than a trochaic or dactylic ending, or to put it in less traditional terms, a final stress suggests greater seriousness than when the last stress is on the penultimate or an earlier syllable. The frequent use of the unstressed ending by the Elizabethan and Jacobean verse dramatists accounts for much of the apparent conversationality that marks their work.

Midway between these options is what's usually called the weak ending, an anapestic or iambic ending with less than full stress on the accent. This also tends to carry a suggestion of conversationality, but without risking the sense of lightness sometimes created by completely unaccented endings:

> I thought you sent the money in.

This was a favorite device of Marianne Moore's; it is, with all her syllabics, a purely metrical consideration.

The omission of what would be a final unaccented syllable in a regular metrical line, called *truncation* or *catalexis,* is a useful device available to the poet writing in trochaic feet because it helps to avoid the monotony that the trochaic line is likely to produce. "What am I supposed to say?" rather than "What am I supposed to tell him?"

Another option, obviously, is the length of the line itself. Most generalizations about this run into immediate contradictions. It's often said that as the line becomes shorter the poem becomes lighter, but then we have to take into account the fine small poem by Donald Justice, "Poem to Be Read at 3 A.M.," a moving, contemplative piece with one to three stresses per line, and most of Ogden Nash's comic poems, with lines like old fence rails.

What is probably safe to say about line length is that a line longer than six stresses is likely to be broken down in the reader's mind into smaller units, 5-2 or 4-3 or 5-3 or 4-4. It is also probably safe to say that the five-stress line is the most flexible line in English, the one to which most readers come, and with fewest suspicions.

The last contact the poet has with the reader's imagination is in the poem's resolution; because of this, it's a highly important and sensitive moment in the poem's life. There are at least nineteen or twenty means by which a poet can change the reader's expectations so that the ending of a poem seems to be in the natural order of things; some of these function through the line break and changes in line length.

Here as in all talk about poems there are no hard rules. There are principles that, when heeded, will result most of the time in a more effective poem. This is all that rules can mean in poetry; I doubt that they mean more in any art, but this makes the understanding of these principles and the use of them by the poet no less essential.

That said, here are some of those principles relating to closure as function of the line.

A reader will tend to expect the ending of a poem, will tend to feel that it's right that the poem end:

- when a line is noticeably shorter or longer than the established line in the poem;

- when an established pattern of terminal rhyme is modified, or when a pattern is introduced where none had been;
- when there is a shift from runover to end-stopped lines.

There is not space here for examples of these types of closure, but they're easy enough to find in most any anthology of poems from any period.

Much of the difference between verse and prose is found in the line and what it does. Prose "broken down" so that it has an uneven right margin doesn't become verse because the length and ending of a line of verse are not arbitrary; they are contributing parts of an organism, and when a poem is put into paragraph form something of what it does as a poem is lost.

The fact that good works sometimes lie uncertainly in more than one genre doesn't mean that the genres are not real. They are real, and the separate natures of the paragraph, the scene, and the line lie at the root of the distinctions between them. Our understanding of what a poem is starts here.

The Revolution That Gave Us Modern Poetry
Never Happened

*T*here never was a revolution in poetry in English, neither in form nor in content. Poetry has always expressed the sensibility of the age in which it was written, so if sensibilities shift, poetry changes with them, but there are no new social sensibilities. Socially we shift back and forth between closed and open systems, concern with form and concern with content, discipline and freedom. There has always been poetry to express the extremes, but the poetry in each generation from which the next generation of poetry has grown has tended to be a balance between the two; measured, euphonic, dramatic, narrative, and written in the spoken language of the time.

But wait a minute. We know that Gerard Manley Hopkins and Emily Dickinson and Walt Whitman did something in the middle of the nineteenth century to make poetry modern. Then T. S. Eliot and Ezra Pound did something from about 1914 for about twenty-five years or so to make it really modern. And then the Black Mountain poets and the Beats did something in the forties and fifties to make it really, really modern. And then someone did something and made it postmodern. So what did they do? What do we mean by modern when we talk about poetry?

Well, we generally say—people who talk about poetry in English, and especially people who get paid to talk about it, say—that modern poetry is marked in style by freedom, in tone by a forthrightness skewed by irony, and in content by relevance to the real, the phenomenological world. It's recognized by its open forms, its casual soundplay, slant rhyme and rhymes that occur at irregular intervals; by its apparently conversational language, in which the diction of the back street, the scientific laboratory, the bedroom, and the kitchen can seem appropriate and, concomitantly, by its down-to-earth, realistic, even naturalistic content; and by its abiding suggestion that every act contains the seeds of its own defeat. This may leave out some modern poetry, but it's a fair statement of what we most often have in mind when we think of a poem as modern.

If we have any trouble agreeing on positive qualities of modern poetry, we know what it isn't: it isn't that sing-songy, ethereal stuff about rippling streams and dancing flowers that earlier poets wrote. We were taught to think this, but this is wrong. Many of the best poems in what we rightly call the Tradition spoke so naturally in this world's voice, about things so mundane and essential to this world, that we can still hear the voices as ours, or almost ours, and we can still believe what happens in the poem, and still care about it.

I'm not pointing out anything here that we are not already familiar with, but there are fathers who don't know the colors of their children's eyes after sitting across the dinner table from them for years. Our familiarity with our own tradition has for some reason not prevented us from saying without embarrassment that there is a poetry that is modern and a poetry that is not.

Let's start with the middle years of the nineteenth century, around the times of Whitman, Dickinson, and Hopkins, the three poets who have been credited with inventing honesty, teaching us to be conversational and relevant to what matters. But they were not alone in their day.

In 1862 Arthur Hugh Clough wrote in "The Latest Dec-
alogue,"

> Thou shalt not kill; but need'st not strive
> Officiously to keep alive.
> Do not adultery commit;
> Advantage rarely comes of it.
> Thou shalt not steal; an empty feat,
> When it's so lucrative to cheat. . . .

What's not modern here?

In 1850 he wrote in "I Dreamt a Dream," from his long poem
"Dipsychus,"

> Ah well, and yet—dong, dong, dong:
> Do, if you like, as now you do;
> If work's a cheat, so's pleasure, too;
> And nothing's new and nothing's true;
> Dong, there is no God; dong!

What's not modern here?

Robert Browning in 1842 published "Soliloquy of the Spanish Cloister," in which he has the speaker say, as he closes his
speech,

> Blasted lay that rose-acacia
> We're so proud of! *Hy, Zy, Hine.* . . .
> 'St, there's Vespers! *Plena gratiá*
> *Ave, Virgo!* Gr-r-r—you swine!

And the same year, in "My Last Duchess":

> That's my last Duchess painted on the wall,
> Looking as if she were alive. I call
> That piece a wonder, now. . . .

And again the same year, Tennyson published "Ulysses," which includes the lines

> All times I have enjoyed
> Greatly, have suffered greatly, both with those
> That loved me, and alone. . . .

And then,

> my purpose holds
> To sail beyond the sunset, and the baths
> Of all the western stars, until I die.
> It may be that the gulfs will wash us down. . . .

Give him "beyond the sunset"; my point is that his language was alive for his time and has almost in its entirety stayed alive through more than the century that has passed since the writing of the poem.

But let's go on back.

Except for the dialect, which was true to his time and place, what is there in Robert Burns's final words to the mouse in his field that would seem out of place in a poem written this year?

> Still thou are blest compared wi' me!
> The present only toucheth thee:
> But och! I backward cast my e'e
> On prospects drear!
> An' forward though I canna see, I guess an' fear!

That's from 1785, almost two hundred years ago.

Let's go on back another hundred years, almost, to 1681, and listen to Andrew Marvell talking to his mistress:

> I would
> Love you ten years before the flood,

> And you should, if you please, refuse
> Till the conversion of the Jews.
> My vegetable love should grow
> Vaster than empires and more slow;
> An hundred years should go to praise
> Thine eyes, and on thy forehead gaze;
> Two hundred to adore each breast,
> But thirty thousand to the rest. . . .

What would you do to these lines to make them modern? Something, but not very much.

Back another fifty years or so, then, to John Donne in 1633, writing the first of the holy sonnets:

> I run to death, and death meets me as fast,
> And all my pleasures are like yesterday.
> I dare not move my dim eyes any way,
> Despair behind, and death before doth cast
> Such terror. . . .

What would you do to these lines to make them modern?

Back to Shakespeare, then. We don't have to go to the plays to find people talking like people about the world as it is. In the face of those sonnets that have sometimes given poetry a bad name, poems idealizing love and the beloved, lifting them out of our atmosphere and making them abstractions, he tells us in sonnet 130:

> My mistress' eyes are nothing like the sun;
> Coral is far more red than her lips' red;
> If snow be white, why then her breasts are dun;
> If hairs be wires, black wires grow on her head.
> I have seen roses damasked, red and white,

> But no such roses see I in her cheeks;
> And in some perfumes is there more delight
> Than in the breath that from my mistress reeks.
> I love to hear her speak, yet well I know
> That music hath a far more pleasing sound;
> I grant I never saw a goddess go;
> My mistress, when she walks, treads on the ground.
> And yet, by heaven, I think my love as rare
> As any she belied with false compare.

This is 1609. But Shakespeare didn't invent plain talk, irony, and skepticism in poetry. Fifty years earlier Thomas Wyatt wrote about the changes that take place as we grow older, and he did it in so natural a diction, drawn from the full middle of the living speech of his time, that now, after more than four hundred years, we can almost feel—almost—that it was written during our lifetime. Almost. The point is that it takes no revolution in taste, in artistic sensibility, to go from this language and attitude to those of Kenneth Patchen or John Berryman, Ezra Pound or Elizabeth Bishop:

> They flee from me, that sometime did me seek,
> With naked foot stalking in my chamber.
> I have seen them, gentle, tame, and meek,
> That now are wild, and do not remember
> That sometime they put themselves in danger
> To take bread at my hand; and now they range,
> Busily seeking with a continual change.
>
> Thanked be fortune it hath been otherwise,
> Twenty times better; but once in special,

In thin array, after a pleasant guise,
When her loose gown from her shoulders did fall,
And she caught me in her arms long and small,
And therewithall sweetly did me kiss
And softly said, "Dear heart, how like you this?"

And this is not to mention the tone and subject matter of the poetry of Geoffrey Chaucer.

Evolution, of course. Poetry has changed. Language has changed. The furniture of our world has changed. But the poetry written before the Industrial Revolution was shaped not by horses and waterwheels; it was shaped by the human mind. Whatever some may try to tell us, there has been no revolution inside of it.

But what about form? Surely free verse, open form, unstructured, freewheeling poetry is a modern invention. Surely if Walt Whitman, Emily Dickinson, and Gerard Manley Hopkins didn't teach us for the first time to write tough poems in plain talk, then Whitman did break the old chains of pattern and make possible our formal freedoms, cancel the old restrictions, and teach us how to let form follow content. Surely he did not.

Let's look again at what we already know.

We are taught to think of the "old" poetry as written in proscribed patterns of rhyme and meter, strictly set, so that a poet entering one is bound to its pattern until the last line is written.

The Choric Song in Alfred Tennyson's poem "The Lotus-Eaters," which dates from the 1830s, consists of eight stanzas ranging irregularly from eleven to twenty-nine lines in length, with lines of three to eight stresses following one another apparently at random. The rhyme scheme changes with each strophe.

While Whitman threw rhyme away, Tennyson used rhyme,

but his rhymes follow no set pattern, and his lines are as irregular as Whitman's.

So we've had irregular lines, open structures, before. And in blank verse we've had unrhymed poetry. What Whitman did was combine the freedoms, freedom from a set line length and freedom from rhyme, to give us truly open and truly modern verse.

But then what do we do with Coleridge's "Kubla Khan," written in 1797, in which not only does each of the four stanzas differ from the others—including as a third stanza a modified Shakespearian sonnet with both four- and five-stress lines—but the first stanza has no pattern to its rhyme at all and lines varying irregularly from three to four to five stresses?

So we've had irregular line lengths with irregular rhyme, but some rhyme was still there, and it was end rhyme. What Whitman did was abandon rhyme altogether, in combination with irregular line length. That was the formal difference.

But then what are we going to do with William Blake and "The Marriage of Heaven and Hell" in 1790? Constructed as an illuminated manuscript with plants, people, and other creatures crawling and flying among the words, "The Marriage of Heaven and Hell" runs to fifteen pages when it's printed as text alone. Included in this text are complete and independent sections in free verse and even prose poems. This was 60 years before "Leaves of Grass," 130 years before the Imagists, 155 years before the Black Mountain poets and Patchen's picture poems. One hundred thirty-two years before "The Waste Land," it mixes references to exotic philosophies, etymological wordplay based on Hebrew and English, Roman numerals, and mathematics. It moves from an inventory of biblical injunctions to free verse to an anecdote in prose to free verse, and so on. It isn't "The Waste Land," but it's one of the many poems that keep "The Waste Land" from being revolutionary.

But even Blake's poem, clearly a move in the development of poetry in English, a recognizable move toward more open forms, was simply that. John Milton, in 1637, moved in "Lycidas" from a basic five-stress line to a three-stress line whenever he wanted one, according to no formula we can figure, and he rhymed now two lines, now three, four, five, or even six together. It's as if he meant to string together a collection of different stanza forms, adding one or another as the whim struck him. The rhyme scheme *bccb*, which connects lines 2–5, doesn't appear again until lines 31–34. Falling between them are *abcabc*, *aba*, *abab*, and ten end words with no rhyme for them at all.

What is free verse? Is it not poetry in which a reader is unable to predict the length of the next line or the position or nature of the next rhyme sound, if one occurs?

George Herbert wrote "The Collar" in 1633. It has, in its thirty-six lines, line lengths of two, three, four, and five stresses with no discernible pattern and rhyme sets of two, three, and four words, scattered at random except for the tightening to *abab* at the end as a resolving device, as Eliot tightened to a terminal couplet for the resolution of "The Love Song of J. Alfred Prufrock."

For a last example we can go back to 1595, when Edmund Spenser wrote his "Epithalamion," a poem whose twenty-four stanzas include seven distinct verse patterns, introduced according to no discernible plan, and vary from seventeen to nineteen lines in length, with a seven-line resolving stanza.

So where do we look to find the proscriptions of form, tone, and diction that are supposed to have kept our earlier poets in straitjackets of poetic protocol and from which modern poetry freed us? Wherever we look, we find ourselves already there, busy writing poetry that was always modern.

Which is not to say that in general the poetry written today is not different from what has in general been written in the past. Certainly it is. But the differences are matters of degree. And they are sharper when we compare our poetry with the poetry of some periods—say, the neoclassical period—than when we compare it with the poetry of other periods—say, the early seventeenth century. There are fluctuations, and there is a direction in the overall change, but there is nothing radically new in itself.

And there is nothing that is old, in the sense that we are through with it. A part of the good fortune of poetry in English is that while we can find poets in almost every time in the past doing what we mostly do, which is to write after the fashion of such works as "The Love Song of J. Alfred Prufrock," "Sunday Morning," or "After Great Fear a Formal Feeling Comes," we can write as they mostly did, in sonnets and villanelle and sestinas and ballad stanzas, and still write acutely of and for our own days. Because if we have not invented much, we need not have lost very much, and the entire tradition of almost eight hundred years of English literature is still with us. It was always bringing us to where we are, and to wherever we are going, and all the way back it's still there for us to use.

Intuition, Spontaneity, Organic Wholeness, and the Redemptive Wilderness

Some Nineteenth-Century Currents in Modern American Poetry

*I*t's always perilous to talk about schools, movements, groups, or any sort of kinships in recent poetry. Proper perspective comes no faster than what we are looking at recedes into the past, and without that perspective we tend to squint. Even so, it seems to me that the value in understanding what's been going on around us in the past few decades is worth the peril, and it's a simple pleasure to the mind.

My mind has been pleasuring itself for a while with the names and works of a few twentieth-century American poets whose names and works keep wanting to come together in what anthologists of the future may call a group or movement that, if it's ever given a name, might be called the Poets of Intuition or the Anti-rationalists. For now, what's happening is easier to describe than to name, so let me list the distinguishing characteristics of some poets whose common vision has seemed to set them apart. Inasmuch as a view of the world can be analyzed, these are the parts that make up the worldview held in common by this energetic and once influential group of poets, some of whom are very good and all of whom are committed to the truth of the vision they share.

- This is what I have read in their heads, as I have read it in their poems:
- The belief that the natural is good and the unnatural is bad.
- The belief that the closer we are to the primitive, the more in tune we are with the natural.

- The association of the primitive with such qualities as spontaneity, intuition, imagination, "sincerity," organic oneness, and
absolute creative freedom on the part of the writer.

Concomitantly, then, there is a distrust of the rational pro-
cess, technology, objectivity, imitation, and arbitrary divisions.
One who believes in organic unity is likely to be uneasy with the
concept of genre and pleased by prose rhythms in verse and lyri-
cal language in prose. One who gives great credit to the imagination is likely to credit magic and myth also, as the natural
product of imagination, as against reason, and is likely to enjoy
obscurity of statement as the natural condition of magic, myth,
and intuition.

Our history in letters and education, as well as in commerce
and social affairs, has from long before the Industrial Revolution been a story of reverence for the rational processes, objectivity, the drawing of distinctions, invention, technology, and
an increasing removal from the direct influence of nature. We
have been of a mixed mind, as we have loved the exploits of the
individualist and feared the individualist for being that. We do,
as Mignon McLaughlin tells us, honor our living conformists
and our dead troublemakers. Shelley and Antigone do pester us,
but Aristotle as we murkily remember him holds us in thrall.
Common sense. Science. Let us reason together. Make sense.
Hegel is much more welcome in our heads than Nietzsche is,
and we like what Thomas Aquinas did to Jesus.

It seems that such rational processes, such objectivity and
clarity of point, have brought us to turmoil and the edge of di-
saster far greater than the time-sweetened madness at the end of
the seventeenth century, out of which century was brewed the
antidote we call neoclassicism.

It should not be surprising, then, that we had among us a movement in poetry characterized by what seems to have been a reaction against all that the century had come to mean.

Robert Bly set down what amounts to a manifesto of this unnamed movement in the first issue of his magazine called *The Seventies.* In part, he said essentially this:

- Intuition is more to be trusted than reason.
- Leap of association in poetry is to intuition what metaphor is to reason.
- Most modern poets have lost the ability to make such leaps of association.
- Emotion improves poetry, as it brings the release of what is damned up in the reader and makes the reader's mind therefore lighter and more able to leap.
- It is good that distinctions between genre and even between art forms be weakened. It is good that poets like Frank O'Hara leap and make one think of painting, and it is to the discredit of nonleaping poets like John Nims and Karl Shapiro that they do not make us think of painting.
- It is better that poetry give us pleasure of the unconscious through leaps of association rather than pleasure of the conscious through metaphor because pleasure of the unconscious is accompanied by a feeling of the mystery of that pleasure.
- Lorca is right for celebrating the spirit of magic in poetry, which, to quote Lorca, "rejects all the sweet geometry one has learned."
- We have three brains (as suggested by Arthur Koestler), each belonging to a stage of our evolutionary history: the reptile brain, the mammal brain, and the "new brain."
- The reptile brain, designed for physical survival and response

to fear, is symbolized by cold; the mammal brain, characterized by a sense of community, love of women and children,
and brotherhood, is symbolized by warmth; the new brain,
whose function is spiritual understanding, mystical insight,
awareness of self, and pure knowing, is symbolized by light.

- While the contemporary energy flow in the brain, because we
  are living in times of great and constant fear, is into the reptile
  brain, ecology workers, poets, singers, mediators, rock musicians, and many people in the younger generation are trying
  desperately to reverse the contemporary energy flow.

Bly's essay, I think, was an intriguing document, not so much
in its examination of the brain but in setting forth as it did the
things most valued by that family of poets to which Bly truly
belongs: mystery and magic, the contemplative spirit, a mind
that is at the same time intuitive, suprarational, nonutilitarian,
in harmony with the essential stirrings of nature, that expresses
itself in surrealism and obscurity, that knows the self, and that
takes us on the road toward perfection and toward redemption
from fear and passion.

It might be helpful here to exemplify what Bly meant by *leap
of association*. Here is a poem he offered as an example. By Greg-
ory Orr, it's called "Silence."

> The way the word sinks into the deep snow of the page.
> The dead deer lying in the clearing, its head and
> > Antlers transparent.
> The black seed in its brain
> Parachuting toward earth.

The first and best of the American poets of the twentieth century whose work was informed by the elements I have listed was

Theodore Roethke. All the younger members of the group stand in his shadow, or, more properly, in his light. These, as I read them, are A. R. Ammons, David Wagoner (Roethke's student who edited and published Roethke's notebooks), Robert Bly, Galway Kinnell, W. S. Merwin, and later James Wright, Gary Snyder, Larry Lieberman, and the Canadian poet Michael Yates. There are others, certainly, but these are the best known and will serve as a fair list to consider. Along with one other, James Dickey, who nearly but not quite belongs here and who I feel sure would not want to be put here. Dickey is concerned with the possible redemptive power of the primitive experience, but he is far from antirationalist or antitechnological, and while there are elements of pantheism in his work, no one would suggest that he sees the world as one organic whole, actually or ideally. While the poets I have named returned to the primitive order to redeem their humanity, Dickey, I believe, went to the primitive to escape it. Dickey had certainly been influenced, as he told us he had, by Roethke, but that influence led him to his own world. He is not one of these.

The work and the attitudes of these poets immediately invite comparison with those of the nineteenth-century English romantics; there clearly are similarities between the groups. The comparisons are interesting as much for the differences, though, as for the areas of kinship.

The nineteenth-century romantic poet believed in intuition, which was to him a thing privately come to out of a worldview drawn in secret.

His twentieth-century colleague sought ways of borrowing from the Eastern mind intuitions born in the East, as the Eastern philosopher, especially the Zen master, impresses us as

the antithesis of the rational, ambitious, and technological creature.

The nineteenth-century romantic poet revered the primitive, which is to say pastoral.

His twentieth-century colleague revered the wilderness,
which may be, as some writers are, friendly to humans or, as
others are, extremely hostile.

Here, to remind us, is something of intuition as we have
it from the nineteenth century. From Wordsworth's "Tintern
Abbey":

> that serene and blessed mood,
> In which the affections gently lead us on—
> Until, the breath of this corporeal frame
> And even the motion of our human blood
> Almost suspended, we are laid asleep
> In body, and become a living soul;
> While with an eye made quiet by the power
> Of harmony, and the deep power of joy,
> We see into the life of things.
>
> (lines 41 ff.)

And Keats tells us, in "Ode on a Grecian Urn," that

> Heard melodies are sweet, but those unheard
> Are sweeter. . . .

Here is what intuition becomes in the lines of Gary Snyder.
Entitled "Once Only," this is the entire poem, in which intuition
is not discussed but is addressed and drawn upon. The poem
does not defend it, as the nineteenth-century poem might have,
but rather answers it, uses it, and depends upon it.

almost at the equator
almost at the equinox
exactly at midnight
    from a ship
    the full

    moon

in the center of the sky.

                    Sappa Creek near Singapore
                    March 1958

This from "Tree Animals," by Lawrence Lieberman:

Owls
Help us to dream.
They enter our sleeping heads
And hoot. They drop some feathers.

David Wagoner tells us that "the bottom of the mind knows all about zero," and he tells us again, in "Weather Report," how

       frost,
That starry geometry,
Streaks out its axiom:

Here, for backdrop again, is what the nineteenth-century romantic meant by the primitive and the natural for which he longed. From Wordsworth, "The Prelude":

The earth is all before me. With a heart
Joyous, nor scared at its own liberty,
I look about; and should the chosen guide
Be nothing better than a wandering cloud,
I cannot miss my way. I breathe again!

> Trances of thought and mountings of the mind
> Come fast upon me: it is shaken off,
> That burthen of my own unnatural self,
> The heavy weight of many a weary day
> Not mine, and such as were not made for me.

Coleridge, "Work without Hope":

> All Nature seems at work. Slugs leave their lair—
> The bees are stirring—birds are on the wing—
> And Winter slumbering in the open air
> Wears on his smiling face a dream of Spring!

From Shelley, "To a Skylark," of course:

> Hail to thee, blithe Spirit!
> Bird thou never wert,
> That from Heaven, or near it,
> Pourest thy full heart
> In profuse strains of unpremeditated art.

As the golden daffodils, the rainbow in the sky, and the steadfast bright star were inspirations and even spirits to emulate, Shelley ends his poem with an all but obligatory address to the skylark:

> Teach me half the gladness
> That thy brain must know,
> Such harmonious madness
> From my lips would flow
> The world should listen then—as I am listening now.

Here is primitive as the twentieth-century romantic poet understood it and preferred it. It is almost all a wilderness.

Where the nineteenth-century romantic might have wanted to become—or become like—a *bird,* his twentieth-century comrade was as likely to want to be a frog, as in David Wagoner's poem, "The Poets Agree to Be Quiet by the Swamp."

> They hold their hands over their mouths
> And stare at the stretch of water.
> What can be said has been said before:
> Strokes of light like herons' legs in the cattails,
> Mud underneath, frogs lying even deeper.
> Therefore, the poets may keep quiet.
> But the corners of their mouths grin past their hands.
> They stick their elbows out into the evening,
> Stoop, and begin the ancient croaking.

Here is the same transference, from J. Michael Yates:

> I watched the bear too long—until my face became
> that of a bear watching a man. It happened with the
> salmon as well: my lower jaw grew into a great hook,
> a hump rose on my back, I reddened until I look like
> fire under the water on my way upstream. I'm waiting
> at the stream-side, claw under the current. Around
> rocks, through the shallows, back out of the water,
> decaying, I'll be there, because there is nothing to do
> but arrive.

Here is the bond to nature, the pull of not-human life, as Galway Kinnell feels it in "Night in the Forest":

> 1
> A woman
> sleeps next to me on the earth. A strand
> of hair flows

> from her cocoon sleeping bag, touching
> the ground hesitantly, as if thinking
> to take root.

The frequent harshness, even hostility, of the desired natural world as it has been seen by these late and curiously romantic poets is described by J. Michael Yates in these lines to someone back home:

> Again and again I go away from you and send back
> only words. Where I am is very cold and the ice
> figures I collect for you never, somehow, survive
> the transport. And so these small black tracks
> upon the page. Where you are is too warm for me.
> This message is a map which shows my exact coordinates
> at this moment. Follow it. Try to find me.
> I should like to be here when you arrive,
> but in this weather it is necessary to keep moving.

Galway Kinnell comes to both a redeeming and a damning insight in the same harsh country of the north. He tells it in "The Bear":

> On the third day I begin to starve,
> at nightfall I bend down as I knew I would
> at a turd sopped in blood,
> and hesitate, and pick it up,
> and thrust it in my mouth, and gnash it down,
> and rise
> and go on running.

Harmony with the universe, organic wholeness, is another important part of the worldview of the new poets that they share

with the nineteenth-century romantics. Wordsworth tells us of
it in "My Heart Leaps Up":

> The Child is father of the Man;
> And I could wish my days to be
> Bound each to each by natural piety.

Shelley tells us of it in "Adonais," which was touched of
course by Plato, as Shelley read him:

> He is a portion of the loveliness
> Which once he made more lovely: he doth bear
> His part, while the one Spirit's plastic stress
> Sweeps through the dull dense world, compelling there
> All new successions to the forms they wear. . . .

And Keats, in "Endymion":

> Feel we these things?—that moment have we stepped
> Into a sort of oneness, and our state
> Is like a floating spirit's.

Gary Snyder says it too, in "Song of the Slip":

> On the dark shoal
> seed-prow
> moves in and makes home in the whole.

J. Michael Yates tells us, "Only I and the mountain aren't
between the mountain and me," and tells us again, "my name is
Nothing; I contain all time and all space."

It does seem that in important moments in the poems of
these later writers, much of Wordsworth and Coleridge, Byron,
Keats, and Shelley, and Blake too, Lander, and Scott if you read

closely, has remained with us, the same but of course not the same. Here are three small poems to say so. The first is an untitled section of *Great Bear Lake Meditations,* by J. Michael Yates.

> I no longer believe in what I don't know about
> cities, but there's still something in open country
> and clear deep water that draws me. Because I fear
> to know: knowledge of something attractive only in
> its enigma is terrible. That sweet small darkness is
> going away as I return and return and cannot but return.
> I turn to this tangled landscape as a man turns to a
> woman and dream that because I haven't been here before,
> neither has any other man.

By James Wright, a poem called

TODAY I WAS SO HAPPY, SO I MADE THIS POEM

As the plump squirrel scampers
Across the roof of the corncrib,
The moon suddenly stands up in the darkness,
And I see that it is impossible to die.
Each moment of time is a mountain.
An eagle rejoices in the oak trees of heaven,
Crying
This is what I wanted.

And from Jo McDougall, two real moments, each reshaped by a romantic mist.

STRANGERS IN THIS CITY WHERE WE HAVE COME
SEEKING A CURE FOR HER CANCER,
MY DAUGHTER AND I DRIVE UP TO THE CLINIC

A buzzard lands on the roof.
In the dusk, in my confusion,

I mistake it for a blue
heron. I call to my daughter, "Look!"

OAKS

When friends came,
bringing food and sympathy,
I asked them to speak of my daughter
In the present tense.

When I visited her grave,
the oak trees,
casting their ferny shadows,
set me straight.

Now McDougall lets a romantic mist be blown away by a pedestrian moment.

A BOTTOMLANDS FARMER SUFFERS
A SEA CHANGE

A man fits a key into the door of an office in Chicago.
Suddenly he remembers a plowed field.
He remembers the farm
before they took it.
He remembers walking its ditches,
flushing birds.

In a park across the street
pigeons scatter.
He hurries into the office
where a phone is ringing.

Here are the final two stanzas of "Lines Written in Early Spring" by Wordsworth, one of McDougall's friends.

The budding twigs spread out their fan,
To catch the breezy air;
And I must think, do all I can,
That there was pleasure there.

If this belief from Heaven be sent,
If such be Nature's holy plan,
Have I not reason to lament
What man has made of man?

Categories—schools, movements, groups—are as perilous as they are tempting, of course. But we continue to shape
them because they seem to be useful, because they help us to see
the relationships between our faces and fashions and recurrent
faiths as we move through decades and centuries. And this, useful or not, remains a pleasure to the mind.

A Case for Rhyme and Meter

*F*or many years now people who have cared enough for poetry to argue about it have been in sometimes heated debate, those who prefer so-called formal poetry on one side and those who prefer so-called free verse on the other. I qualify the labels because all good poetry, including free verse, is structured in essential ways, but for the purposes of what I want to say here we can use the term *formal,* as most do, to mean poetry with a set metrical pattern and usually with rhyme, and call everything else free verse.

For a while it seemed as if the use of rhyme and meter had fallen into such disrepute that there would soon be no one writing formal poetry. At a gathering in the late sixties ambitiously called the "First World Poetry Conference" the Canadian poet Stanley Cooperman was booed for reading a poem in rhymed quatrains.

The cogs of history, though, are constantly turning. Over the past few years an increasing number of younger poets have joined the few older ones who all this time continued to write in rhyme and meter, and it seems now to have become respectable again.

Still, with so little serious discussion of prosody taking place in or out of the classroom over the past years, many poets who might find their work enriched by rhyme and meter may not even know what it is they're missing. I have a few things to say that I hope will help to change that.

Let me turn first to a couple of the stock arguments against the use of metrical patterns and rhyme: that it makes the language of a poem artificial and that paying attention to the mechanics of a poem distracts a poet from the flow of language, restricting free expression and cooling the necessary passion of the act of poetry.

Artificial? Of course the patterns of poetry are artificial. All art is artifice wrestling with ordinary life; all discussion of art is at heart a discussion of the relationship between the artificial and the natural.

A distraction, a restriction, an intrusion of the mechanical upon the passions? Absolutely. Robert Frost was asked once by a woman at a writers' conference whether, when he was writing his beautiful poems, he really paid attention to all those technical things. "Madam," he replied, "I revel in them." William Blake cautioned us to bear in mind that "without minute neatness of execution, the sublime cannot exist," that "singular and particular detail is the foundation of the sublime." I wrote once to the poet Fred Chappell, after reading one of his fine and patterned poems in a journal, to say how rare it was to find soul and precision so well married. That is the essence of all art, that marriage.

Specifically, a formal pattern gives the statement of a poem something to push out against. Much of the energy in a good poem with a pattern comes from the tension created when a statement that wants to run on and spread out, to take over the page, is held in check and given shape by the poem's form, the way a cylinder contains and focuses the fuel's explosion in an internal combustion engine, the way those inflexible curves and immovable holes of the saxophone got in the way of John Coltrane. Without those restrictions there is nothing but wind.

A pattern also gives the *poet* something to move against. The

closing line of Clement Long's "For a Skydiver Knocked Unconscious by Another" is strengthened as a resolution because it
won't let go of us when we expect it to.

> She didn't cry out. There wasn't enough time.
> In that small conscious space after she saw
> The ground, once far and featureless, suddenly there,
> Her body twisted as if she were trying to climb
> Back into the clouds. There was time to claw
> At sunlight, to hunt a foothold in the bright and useless
>   air.

The first five lines of the poem are in fairly regular pentameter,
mostly iambic, with five stresses per line; the sad final line holds
onto the reader for six stresses, one more than expected, driving
the horror home, as if we saw the doomed skydiver in slow motion. The effect would not be so strong, our expectations would
not be undone, if those expectations had not been established
by the poem's measured lines. In unmeasured verse this effect
would have been unavailable to the poet.

The answer to both these objections—that form is artificial
and that it's a distraction—lies in the realization that everything going on in a poem has the effect of moving it along a line
between pure ritual and plain talk. Define ritual as a human activity that follows a known pattern, mainly for the symbolism in
the pattern itself, as in an initiation rite or a high requiem mass.
The more a poem is like a ritual, the more difficult it is for us
as readers to believe that it's a part of our lives, that it has to do
with the world we have to survive in; the closer it is to ordinary
talk, the less interest we have in it as art. The poet's job is to fix
the poem at just the right point on that line, the right point for
that poem and for the distance we ought to stand from it.

The means of moving a poem one way or the other lie in the

manipulation of diction, syntax, figures of speech, end stopping, rhythms and meter, and rhyme. Latinate or a more formal diction (*spirit* rather than *ghost, paternal* rather than *fatherly*), simple syntax (with short sentences and few subordinate clauses), frequent metaphors and other figures of speech, strong end stopping, a regular metrical pattern and regular, true rhyme all tend to heighten the reader's sense of ritual in a poem. End stopping, meter, and rhyme are the formal elements among these variables, those that most emphatically make a poem other than free verse. Without them, especially without rhyme and meter, a poet's flexibility in moving back and forth between the poles of ritual and talk is severely limited, as if the poet were left writing on only one side of the page.

Here are two short poems of my own, the first relatively close to plain talk, the second closer to pure ritual, the difference being primarily in the uses of end stopping, meter, and rhyme:

AESTHETIC DISTANCE

The moon is dark. We have our drinks on a terrace
on Gianicolo hill. There is a little war
in the streets of Rome. We see the flashes from pistols,
the sweeping lights, we hear the pistols popping.
We watch a Molotov cocktail burning its curve.
"Star bright," somebody says. "Make a wish."

DEAD SONG FOR A NEIGHBOR CHILD
WHO RAN AWAY TO THE WOODS

She finally found a place they couldn't find.
She wouldn't come if she could hear them call.

She knew love tore at the flesh, and flesh was all.
Stilled in breeze-blown stems and out of mind

she rode the buzzing summer, fretful fall.
She finally found a place they couldn't find.
She wouldn't come if she could hear them call.
Safe at last, unfeeling, deaf, and blind,
she lay past even peace, where countless small
and many-legg'd and legless creatures crawl.
She finally found a place they couldn't find.
She knew love tore at the flesh, and flesh was all.

To be able to use rhyme and meter and all the other devices of poetry is simply to have in hand the tools of the trade. For a saddle maker, a chef, or an airplane mechanic that would be argument enough; it seems to me that it would be for anyone doing anything, but there's still an argument to be made. First, about rhyme in particular.

Rhyme always enhances the enjoyment we get from the music of a poem and especially from the pairing of near identities, unfailingly a pleasure to the mind. We like to see or hear together or in close sequence pairs or larger sets of objects or colors or sounds that are nearly but not quite the same. The king and queen on the chessboard are more pleasant to behold than two kings or two queens; a sweater on a red-headed woman, if it's a shade more rusty than her hair, gives us more pleasure than it would if it were exactly the same shade; a musical chord gives us more pleasure than the sound of three horns all playing the same note.

In the same way, *weight* and *freight,* or *islands* and *silence* (the second pair all the more for being slant rhymes), afford us more enjoyment than *freight* and *freight* or *silence* and *silence* and a lot more than *islands* and *freight.*

Beyond all this, rhyme is useful because it increases the difficulty in the writing of a poem. This may seem a strange thing to say, but as John Ciardi pointed out to us, we could make the goalposts wider, the cups on the golf course bigger and closer together, the baskets on a basketball court larger and lower, but if we did, we would diminish the joy in playing and watching. Much of the point of any human activity not aimed at physical survival lies in its difficulty. The reason we can stand in awe of a poem's pattern laid down by Richard Wilbur or Donald Justice is that we can see the challenges they set for themselves and how well they met them.

So the fullest pleasure in any writing requires the greatest challenges. The fullest pleasure in the reading of a poem requires an awareness of the challenges the poet accepted, one of which may have been to set rhymes in place without contorting the natural flow of the language.

Even beyond this, rhyme can allow us to communicate in two ways at once. This is the rhetorical use of rhyme, by which the rhyme becomes a part of the statement the poem makes.

In my poem "Fred," the one rhyme sound belongs to him, rhymes with his name, until his wife knows that she's free of him.

FRED

Taking a husband's duties to heart
he kept her decently dressed and fed

and everything had seemed alright
till pissed again by something she said

and truly believing in the right
he whomped her up aside of the head

the way he had for all the years
they'd shared a table and a bed.

To his surprise she didn't cry
but turned and walked away instead,

went upstairs and got his gun,
took careful aim and shot him dead.

She stood with neither grin nor frown
and gazed upon him while he bled.

She managed to get him into a chair
and got herself a needle and thread

and closed the hole in the cambric shirt.
Then she got some jelly and bread

and milk and tuned the TV
to something she'd often wanted to see.

The rhymes in my poem "Morning at the Zagorsk Monas-
tery outside Moscow" reflect the heavy-handed, lockstep culture that shaped an old woman's thoughts, adding a sad irony to
her deprecation of Stalin. A few lines of this poem are enough to
make the point.

I say a prayer
for poor Joseph Stalin, for all those years
when he was there
in every mirror, in every telephone.
He comes in dreams,
bloody and torn, dripping with remorse,
or so it seems.
Who knows what is actual on this earth?
Nevertheless,
what it comes to, poor God being dead,

is saying yes.
That is what I say. It's what I've said
these awful years.
I don't see any point at all now
in spending tears
On those that haven't said it. Let them lie.
I almost grieved
once for old Stalin, who I suppose
truly believed
there wasn't any God, and now he knows.

One of the little-noted and most overlooked advantages of rhyme is the way in which it broadens the poet's net for language. The search for a rhyme leads a poet not infrequently to come across words that otherwise would not have been considered for the poem at hand and that in turn can take the poem in delightfully surprising directions.

Rhyme also allows us to put a point on a joke that would be impossible without it. We can imagine the loss of sting in this small poem by Howard Nemerov if it were not rhymed as it is:

STRANGE METAMORPHOSIS OF POETS

From epigram to epic is the course
For riders of the American wingèd horse.
They change both size and sex over the years,
The voice grows deeper and the beard appears;
Running for greatness they sweat away their salt,
They start out Emily and wind up Walt.

Rhyme also allows us to encapsulate, to be epigrammatic. It would be interesting to try changing the rhyme words in the following poems and see what happens, how flaccid the poems become.

> And what is love? Misunderstanding, pain,
> Delusion, or retreat? It is in truth
> Like an old brandy after a long rain,
> Distinguished, and familiar, and aloof.
> > —J. V. Cunningham

THE COMMON WISDOM

> Their marriage is a good one. In our eyes
> What makes a marriage good? Well, that the tether
> Fray but not break, and that they stay together.
> One should be watching while the other dies.
> > —Howard Nemerov

LOVE AND DEATH

> And yet a kiss (like blubber)'d blur and slip,
> Without the assuring skull beneath the lip.
> > —John Nims

A part of what would be lost without the rhymes is the mnemonic quality of the poems, the ease with which they are committed to memory. Sometimes a few friends and I have fallen into a fit of quoting poems to one another, anyone's poems, from Thomas Wyatt to Maxine Kumin, Robert Herrick to Al Young, until all but one of us has run out of memory. It's what jazz musicians call a "cutting session." Except for Dylan Thomas's "Fern Hill" and the first section of Allen Ginsberg's "Howl," I don't recall anyone quoting at length from an unrhymed poem.

Occasionally a poet will choose to build the sound structure of a poem on identities rather than rhyme, as in this stanza from my "Ghosts":

> If pity comes, don't let it go to them.
> Watch for a sudden change in temperature.
> You still have a death to deal with.
> Pity yourself, who could be one of them.

And in this one from Reed Whittemore's "For the Life of Him and Her":

> For the life of her she couldn't decide what to wear to the
>   party.
> All those clothes in the closet and not a thing to wear.
> Nothing to wear, nothing wearable to a party.
> Nothing at all in the closet for a girl to wear.

The poet is aiming in such cases at a special effect, a sense of returning in sound not almost but precisely to where you were, creating a difficulty in moving forward and an increased removal from reality.

In the following poem Gwendolyn Brooks does both; that is, she establishes a regular rhyme scheme and a pattern of terminal repetition that work together, giving us two simultaneous patterns that create a kind of chant, a strongly ritualist movement, as if the things these pool players are saying can be constrained enough for comprehension by nothing less than two forms at once, one inside the other. And look at the effect of the absence of *we* in the last line, purely because we had come to expect it.

WE REAL COOL
THE POOL PLAYERS.
SEVEN AT THE GOLDEN SHOVEL.

We real cool. We
Left school. We

Lurk late. We
Strike Straight. We

Sing sin. We
Thin gin. We

Jazz June. We
Die soon.

The sestina, probably the most popular form built on word repetition instead of rhyme, builds a pattern for the poet to play upon in some interesting ways. Here are the beginning lines of my sestina "Love in the Cathedral":

> In the beginning I couldn't speak to you.
> Not because the words wouldn't come;
> it was because they might. Not words like love,
> blooming where they fall; words like come here.
> When once you turned to look straight at me
> out of a crowd, I thought I must have let
>
> the sounds inside my head come out. . . .

The prescribed rotation of the repeated final words, stanza by stanza, is such that these words in the last nine lines of the poem carry their own message:

> No matter what may come,
> give me this: that all this time I stood here
> ignored to death and loved you while you let
> every chance go; say your glances at me
> suggested almost anything but love;
> say I know you cried in bed, poor you.
>
> Believe in love. You know that I am here
> to let you loose. Here is my flesh for you
> who may abide with me till kingdom come.

Not particularly aesthetic. *Brick* and *Brick* may say something to us, but the pairing probably does not stir in most people a sense of pleasure in the repeated sounds.

Finally, all the elements come together in a poem's resolution, in the way it closes down. A reader will know that a poem is over, of course, when there is no more print to be read, but if the poem is not properly resolved it will feel as if the floor has suddenly fallen away. Many of the means of resolving a poem lie in the handling of form and the expectation that form has raised: the introduction of a longer or shorter line than expected, a tightening of the poem's established meter, modification of the rhyme pattern, returning to a rhyme scheme or stanza form after deviating from it. Without the expectations that form raises some of the best means of resolution are lost.

Now and then those who argue for the greater effectiveness of free verse have pointed to T. S. Eliot's "The Love Song of J. Alfred Prufrock," perhaps the most important single poem of our century written in English, as an example of how powerful free verse can be. It is, in fact, an example of how effectively a good poet can disguise established patterns. "Prufrock" is not free verse but tightly metrical blank verse with the five-stress lines frequently broken into two or three feet or one and four feet, these scattered about the poem, with scattered rhyme throughout, and with the standard blank-verse resolving device (as in Shakespeare's scenes) of a terminal rhymed couplet. I recommend this very sort of thing, experimenting with set forms—ballad stanzas, sonnets, heroic quatrains, whatever—as a rewarding way to rediscover the forms and the good uses of pattern in poetry.

Not every worthy poem is written in rhyme and meter. There are poems in free verse for which I'm truly grateful, and I've written some that I'm rather pleased with. But all of the poet's tools are there for us to use, and I can't think of any reason not to use them when the raw material of subject and tone calls for them.

I want to let my friend Nicanor Parra, the wise and irascible Chilean poet, resolve these few observations with a little poem (in my translation) that tells us, however we choose to write, what we mustn't forget.

YOUNG POETS

Write as you will
In whatever style you like.
Too much blood has run under the bridge
To go on believing
That only one road is right.

In poetry everything is permitted.

With only this condition, of course:
You have to improve on the blank page.

Acknowledgments

"We Real Cool," by Gwendolyn Brooks, is from *Blacks* (Chicago: Third World Press, 1991). © 1991 by Gwendolyn Brooks.

"And what is love? Misunderstanding, pain," by J. V. Cunningham, is from *The Exclusion of a Rhyme* (Athens: Ohio University Press, Swallow Press, 1960). © 1960 by J. v. Cunningham. Printed with the permission of the author.

"The Common Wisdom" and "Strange Metamorphosis of Poets," by Howard Nemerov, are from *The Western Approaches* (Chicago: University of Chicago Press, 1975). © 1975 by Howard Nemerov.

"Love and Death," by John Nims, is from *Selected Poems* (Chicago: University of Chicago Press, 1982). © 1982 by John Nims.

"Young Poets," by Nicanor Parra, is from *Poems and Antipoems* (New York: New Directions, 1966). © 1966 by Nicanor Parra. Used by permission of New Directions Publishing Corporation.

"Aesthetic Distance," by Miller Williams, is from *The Boys on Their Bony Mules* (Baton Rouge: Louisiana State University Press, 1983). © 1983 by Miller Williams.

"Dead Song for a Neighbor Child" and "Fred," by Miller Williams, are from *Points of Departure* (Urbana and Chicago: University of Illinois Press, 1995). © 1995 by Miller Williams.

"For a Skydiver Knocked Unconscious by Another," by Clement Long, © 1995. Used by permission.

The Value of Poetry in a Technological Age

$\mathcal{W}$e are increasingly and ironically insulated from one another by our very means of communication.

This is not entirely new to us. When the telegraph first allowed us to convey the printed word quickly over great distances, we had to read without recognizing the steady or uneasy hand of the sender, the sprawling letter of a child, or the consolingly familiar handwriting of an absent parent.

When the telephone first allowed us to speak and hear over great distances, we had to learn to talk and listen without seeing the hint of a smile or pain in the eyes.

So our separation by what connects us is not very recent if we measure by the length of a human life, but the technology that brings this about pervades our culture now to such a degree that the quantitative difference has become a qualitative difference. Three generations in my family communicate with friends, relatives, and colleagues around the world by Internet and fax. We have to be mindful that a granddaughter's e-mail girlfriend in Tucson may not be a girl or a friend.

We call an 800 number to complain or get information and have to work our way through an electronic decision tree hoping for an unrecorded voice eventually.

A comedian tells us, "Have your machine call my machine."

Teenagers (and sometimes their parents) compete at electronic games on the television or computer screen, no longer facing one another.

I'm not sure what the eventual effect of all this will be. I do know that isolation from actual human contact, carried to the extreme, can be destructive to body and mind, as it is in solitary confinement.

But now let me confess something to you: I like this technology, most of it. I'm comfortable with it. I like to race along a hard disk in search of a lost icon, I enjoy fax and e-mail, and I sometimes play games against my computer late at night.

Still, we cannot ignore the likelihood that the more we communicate with and through machines, the greater the danger of losing touch with our human selves. However much we have come to need our technology, we need more. We need balance, and the sanity that balance implies.

We hear that we are in a postliterate age, that the written word for its own sake no longer has a place in our culture, that literature as we have known it is an anachronism; that poetry, certainly poetry, will have no relevance and no place in the new world.

But no—just the opposite is true. There has never been a day when poetry was more important. In a time of high technology we need more, not less, to be in touch with that part of ourselves we call the human spirit.

There can be a luminous beauty in science and technology, but if that is our only means of communicating with others and with ourselves, we are alone together.

And technology raises a concern besides the insulation it can place around us. Some of the processes that take place within us require more time than microchips like to allow. As we move into an era when speed of accomplishment is a measure of value, we need more, not less, to find a time to slow down, to take into ourselves the sound of a symphony as we move at its pace, and not it at ours; to stand in front of a painting, to walk around a piece of sculpture, long enough to comprehend it; to read a poem fully, as a participant in its making. To slow down.

Partly as a result of the technological changes that are taking place, much of the social landscape is also shifting. Old standards, old signposts, structures, conventions, and principles that have held for hundreds and even thousands of years have come to seem less certain, less dependable, no longer appropriate or believable or useful. It's hard, and becoming harder, to know for sure what a family is, what normal is, what freedom is, or space, or life.

When we can custom-design genetic properties and call into question even the material nature of the universe, in a time when many of those patterns that have given shape to our lives are disappearing or becoming difficult to recognize, when perhaps more than ever before our culture seems chaotic, we need more, not less, to have some order in our daily existence.

Humanity has a rage for company and for order.

Just as we have to have actual contact with other human beings to stay sane, we have to have order in our lives, in our minds. As it becomes difficult to find this in the old structures, it is always there to be found in the arts. In poetry, for instance.

Writing Your Own Poem

*T*he author Thomas Campbell in the early 1850s penned to a young lady who had asked him to write something original in her album:

> how should I begin?
> For I fear I have nothing original in me
> Excepting Original Sin.

Campbell was pretending modesty, of course; his very observation is highly original, and he knew it was. He also knew that it was important to be original, not to seem a parrot repeating another poet's phrases. It's still important, and because so much has been written down since the early nineteenth century, it's even more difficult for us than it was for Thomas Campbell not to write what has already been written, sometimes written over and over again. It is difficult, and it ought to be difficult, or there would be no value in it, but it is not impossible.

A note of caution:

The wonderfully contorted syntax and luxuriant alliteration of Gerard Manley Hopkins and E. E. Cummings give their poems undeniable distinctiveness, and Cummings was able to follow Hopkins in this way without seeming to copy him too much, but a poet who tries twisting one or both of these poets—using, say, the gimmick of the lowercase *i* as the personal pronoun—will be seen as so obviously mimicking that any serious reader will likely stop reading at that point.

Much more significant than what Hopkins and Cummings did is the fact that many poets have developed distinctive voices without gimmicks, without distorting the language as it's spoken. Again, exciting and admirable as the poetry of Hopkins and Cummings is, it comes from an alchemy that can't be repeated without doing what has already been done. Important as their poetry is, it's of greater importance that we can usually recognize the authorship of a poem by John Donne, Emily Dickinson (even without the dashes), Thomas Hardy, Hart Crane, Edna St. Vincent Millay, Langston Hughes, John Crowe Ransom, Elizabeth Bishop, Dylan Thomas, John Ciardi, Charles Bukowski, James Dickey, and countless others whose language in poetry seems as natural as the language we speak, allowing for line breaks, a more controlled rhythm, and heightened soundplay. When the poetry of any of these is read aloud, without affectation, there is a compelling illusion of conversation. There are no gimmicks we can identify. Still, we know which poet's work we are hearing. How does a poet put a hallmark on a work without somehow contorting it, making it seem not quite of the real world?

In other words, how does one find that combination of qualities—cadence, diction, tone, attitude, and form—that will make a poem an original thing, make it one's own? Since no mind is quite like any other, each person who is able to write a poem should be able to write a poem that is not like any other. There is no sure way to make this happen, but here are some suggestions to make it more likely, if they are taken to heart.

- Every act of writing is an excursion into memory. This is especially true of poetry. Make sure that it's your memory into which you travel, and not someone else's. Even if the events

in the poem involve an invented character, the emotions surrounding what happens and what the imagination does with
those events must come from your own history of abuse or
contentment, faith or uncertainty, and no one else's. Let the
poem know what you've learned in your life.

- Because imagery is so effective a device in poetry, and because an image gives the reader a very specific touch of detail, poets learning the craft sometimes get the idea that detail
of any kind makes for good poetry. In fact, lines of plain detailed description—of an old building or a field of flowers or
of a mountain range or how one picks strawberries—can be
deadly to a poem and except from the hands of an excellent
writer of prose almost never sounds new to us. One focused
image or one sweeping suggestion will do a lot more to keep
a poem your own than will detailed description. Remember
that suggestion always triggers the imagination; description
almost never does.

- Read contemporary poetry and read a great deal in what we
call poetry of the tradition. You can't avoid doing what's been
done if you don't know what's been done. It was probably un-
necessary to say that, because surely anyone who cares enough
about poetry to try to write it cares enough about it to read
it, for the love of it. To want to write poetry without having a
compulsion to read it is unimaginable.

- In the most elementary terms, avoid stock adjective-noun
combinations and stale comparisons. These are the bane of
the poet who is learning the craft, the first giveaway of one
who has not found a voice: *bubbling spring, searing heat, bla-
tant lie, limp as a dishrag, sharp as a tack, quick as a wink.*

- Try making your poem a narrative, perhaps a dramatic monologue, rather than the momentary expression of an emotion.

Any story will more probably be one of a kind than a feeling will be.

- Let the tale or the dramatic monologue be about someone other than the poet. This will likely bring you to see things in a new way.

- When you tell a story in a poem, no matter who the protagonist is, no matter who the narrator is, avoid the depiction of any character in the poem as a "good guy" or a "bad guy." Every believable character is complex, and complexity is never a copy of another complexity.

- One way not to write the poetry of the past is to write clearly of the present. Be contemporary, then, but don't be so much of today that your work will be stale tomorrow. A poem that speaks of four-wheel drive or a skateboard will have a freshness about it, and so will a poem that speaks of a Honda Accord, but we have to remember that a very few years ago *Packard* and *Studebaker* would have given a poem a contemporary feel but now date a good number of poems. Still, a poem that starts in a checkout line is more likely to go its own way than one that starts in a garden or on a bench.

- Be true to your sense of yourself. Trust who you are, and you will never be mistaken for another. The poet and critic David Baker says much the same thing when he tells his students, "Be faithful to the language you heard when you were growing up; every family has its own way of talking." That's not bad advice for any writer.

- While you are being true to yourself, avoid running on about yourself, and especially avoid intimate revelations. Most readers find these as discomfiting as they would find such confessions at a cocktail party. In spite of what sort of *National Inquirer* splash it may have made for a while, the fact is that confessional poetry is the least fresh of any. What may seem unique to you—the first time you did something or somebody did something to you—is to others one repetition in an endless pattern when it's reported without the distance and perspective we almost never find if the experience is our own. A psychiatrist is paid to hear an endlessly repeated baring of the soul, sometimes lurid, often sad, and nearly always self-indulgent. The reader of poetry is not paid to, and increasingly does not want to, partly because what the poet thinks is new—because it never happened to the poet before—is not new at all to the human race, to which the reader belongs.

- This is not to say that you should not tell a story in the first person. You simply have to be sure that the "I" in the poem—ostensibly you—is so emblematic of humanity that most any reader would assume that role, could be that "I."

- To make this more likely, you have to free yourself from bondage to the facts. You will always start a poem with a germ of something that really happened, but if the poem is to be your own and no one else's you have to work some invention through and around the facts. Poetry is not journalism; it's an art form, and as John Ciardi paraphrased Picasso, "A poem lies its way to the truth." To paraphrase John Ciardi, in turn, a poem has to invent its way to originality.

- Finally, the poem has to sound interesting, because what is interesting is obviously not imitative or warmed over. It's important to read each poem over, aloud, to work on the words until the sounds of the poem read aloud are satisfying, until they would be a pleasure to someone who didn't understand the language.

All this can make a poem new, but newness is not everything.

If you can keep all these suggestions in mind, and if you can get outside yourself to read and hear what you write as if you were a stranger to the writer, and if you can be honest about what you would tell the writer, you may or may not write poems that work, but if they fail, it won't be for lack of originality. You will have to look for some other reason. There are plenty of them, which is why the simple act of writing a poem can be so difficult and why it is so deeply rewarding.

Translate

L. *Trans,* across: *latus,* borne. To transfer, to carry across, esp. from one language to another.

*W*ork in the English language is traditionally either in creative writing or in scholarship. Translation is the wedding of creative writing and scholarship. This makes it a uniquely demanding and challenging field to work in, but it has caused it also to be over the centuries a much misunderstood, mistrusted, and often badly practiced field.

It was until the 1960s very difficult to publish work in translation except in the few cases of major foreign books, whose rendering into English was sometimes commissioned by a publishing house, and translators were generally looked upon as little more than clerks. Since about 1960, though, translation has begun to come into its own.

Several journals now are devoted exclusively to translated works, and most journals carry some. A growing number of colleges offer workshops in translation. And so now American college students whose parents knew Frost and Eliot and Auden and Robison and Jeffers and maybe something of García Lorca, Cervantes, and Dostoevsky not only know these but also know Borges and Voznesenski, Neruda, Akhmatova, Machado, Quasimodo, Ungaretti, Parra, and Páz. This is as it should be, but there is a problem. While a reader learns to tell the difference between a good and a bad poem or between a good and a bad story, we tend to take a translation as a translation, without passing judgment or even knowing quite what to demand of it. This is the order of things, I suppose; poetry also was made for a long time before it was viewed with a critical eye. But there are special dangers in a critical ignorance toward translation. A poem carried over clumsily from another language is not simply a bad poem in English; it is a misrepresentation of the original poem. It is a fraudulent document.

This is to say something about what happens when we carry a poem from one language to another. We have to understand first, of course, that the translation of a poem is not the simple restatement of the poem's rational content into a second language. Robert Frost, who did not trust translation, possibly because his poetry was never well translated, told us that poetry was what was left behind in translation, but if what a translator carries across to the reader of the second language is everything but the poetry, he carries across very little. It hardly seems worth it. Here is an example of that sort of rendering from *The Penguin Book of Spanish Verse,* in which the publisher acknowledges that the English translations are prose. These are the last lines of "Salmo por el Hombre de Hoy," by Blas de Otero. Even if your Spanish is not fluent, you can hear the poetry in the language.

> Míra, Señor, que tanto llanto, arriba,
> en pleamar, oleando a la deriva,
> amenaza cubrirnos con la Nada.
>
> ¡Ponnos, Señor, encima de la muerte!
> ¡Agoganta, sosten neustra, mirada
> para que aprenda, desde ahora, a verte!

Here is what we are given as "Psalm for Contemporary Man":

> See, O Lord, that so much weeping up there, at high
> water, giving extreme unction as it drifts, threatens
> to overlay us with nothingness.

> Raise us, O Lord, above death. Extend and support
> our gaze so that it may learn henceforth to see you.

Now, if we heard this as a prayer in church, we might say that it was a middling good prayer. It is no more than that, and no one is going to slow down much to hear it.

It may be possible for a prayer to be no more than its rational meaning, but we cannot separate a poem from the reader's emotional and imaginative response to it. A poem is what a poem does to us and draws from us. Going through a poem with a dictionary, word by word, will not help us very much. *Dios mio* cannot be carried over as *my God,* because *Dios mio* does to the Spanish-speaking reader more what *good Lord* does to us.

A translator must be faithful, then, to the effect of a poem, the texture of the line, the level of diction, the tone of voice, and, to the extent possible, the form in which the original poem was written. And the translator into English must be faithful at the same time to the nature of the English language.

This calls for a constant balance of compromises, of course. Sometimes we're lucky, as I clearly was in translating the following lines from the Spanish of the Chilean poet Enrique Lihn. Lihn is describing a rooster crowing at his window in the morning, with the sun behind it:

> Se limita a aullar como un hereje en la hoguera de sus
>   plumas.
> Y es el cuerno gigante
> que sopla la negrura al caer al infierno.

In direct English it is remarkably the same thing:

> He howls like a heretic in the bonfire of his feathers.
> He is a gigantic horn blowing the darkness to hell.

Not many lines translate themselves so nicely. In the poem "Madrigal" Nicanor Parra says, "Ya me he quemado bastante las pestañas / En esta absurda carrera de caballos." This says literally, "I have already burned my eyelashes enough in this absurd horse race," but even if the language were credible in English, what reader of English is going to understand what is meant by having burned one's eyelashes? The line in Spanish is drawn from the more common expression *quemarse las cejas,* which means to overexert oneself, to try until it hurts.

I wanted a line that not only meant the same thing in English as the line in Spanish but was equally colloquial. I wanted to say what Parra might have said had English been his language. My first line was, "I've already burned enough midnight oil." It was a bad try. For one thing, it wasn't as strong as the Spanish line, didn't have the sense of urgency it needed. For another, it was too impersonal; the Spanish line referred to a part of the speaker's body. *Midnight oil* made me think of whales. So how about "I have already busted my gut enough"? Better, but the line didn't sound natural. We don't ordinarily use *already* with *enough* in this contest. So I dropped *already,* which left me with "I've busted my gut enough in this absurd horse race." It was almost something I could live with. I think it does to the reader in English very much what the original lines do to a reader in Spanish, except that *absurd* is a little too proper for the first part of the line. What I wanted was *stupid:* "I've busted my gut enough in this stupid horse race."

Clearly, I was able to carry across less of Parra's lines than I was of Enrique Lihn's passage about the rooster and the bonfire. With Parra's lines I had to make a choice that, because of the fortuitous conjunction of sound and sense, I was not obliged to make with Lihn's passage. When a choice has to be made between being faithful to a poem's words and being faithful to its effect, faithfulness to the word is the worst of infidelities.

There are times when one wants to give up on a translation. I came to such a moment when I was working on Antonio Machado's "La Muerte del Nino Herido" (Death of the Injured Child).

> —Duermes, oh dulce flor de sangre mia?
> El cristal del balcon repíquetéa.
> —Oh fria, fria, fria, fria, fria!

In immediate English this reads:

> Do you sleep, sweet flower of my blood?
> The balcony window playfully repeats your words—
> Cold, cold, cold, cold, cold!

Now, there is an awful irony in the Spanish. *Repíquétéar* does mean "to chime in a festive way"; children at play might make sounds something like *fria, fria, fria, fria, fria*. And this is the *fria,* the cold of the child's death. But in English, what happy children at play made sounds like *cold, cold, cold, cold, cold?* I have not yet figured a way to render the experience plus the meaning—that is, both the sound and the sense—of this passage. This is the sort of problem that keeps a translator awake, but there's joy even in the frustration of it.

We tell great stories of this frustration, and of the joy. The story of Jean Champollion and the Rosetta Stone, for instance: When thirty-two-year-old Champollion, after years of work, finished translating the first element of the Rosetta Stone, he yelled, "I've got it!" and passed out at his desk. He was dead a decade later. Fifty years later, George Smith shouted, after deciphering a cuneiform tablet, "I'm the first person to read this after two thousand years of oblivion!" He began tearing off his clothes. He translated nothing else and died at thirty-six.

Such a story makes translation seem a perilous if rewarding activity, and I would not do anything to disabuse you of that impression. There is a richness in English that makes translating into it particularly both perilous and rewarding. Our history has brought us into such contact with French and with Anglo-Saxon that English itself is bilingual, or more properly, biradical. We have both Latinate and Teutonic words for almost everything. About 75 percent of our written language is Latin in origin, and the other 25 percent is for the most part Teutonic; in our spoken language the division is about 50-50. This accounts, in part, for the greater formality of written English.

When the Norman conquerors imposed their ways on the Anglo-Saxon inhabitants of England, they insisted that their language—French—be spoken in their presence. They were present in the marketplace, in the courtroom, in the classroom, in the dining room; they were not generally within earshot in the bedroom, the bathroom, the kitchen, and the barnyard. So that even today a beast we learned to call a *cow* when the conqueror was not around is called *beef*—his word—when it is placed upon the table. Quite naturally, our associations with those words we used with our families and friends in our less invaded places were warmer, deeper, and more evocative. Compare the words in these pairs—called synonyms by the head but not by the heart—in which the first word is Latinate in origin, the second Anglo-Saxon: *maternal/motherly, manually / by hand, oculist / eye doctor, lactate / give milk, rhythm/beat, altitude/height, liberty/freedom, spirit/ghost, mortality/death, vivacious/lively.*

A translator into English must deal with every sentence, every phrase, every word, as a set of options none of which is perfectly right. No wonder that John Ciardi called translation the art of failure. But if every attempt to translate does finally end in failure, this is not because we're translating; it's because we're using language. There is no word in any language that says what we mean it to say. Those who attack the possibility of translation are in fact attacking language itself. It is not when we begin to translate that we begin to fail; it is when we begin to use words.

Whether or not we mean to dissimulate, we do. Not only because *libertad, freedom,* and *freiheit* do not mean the same thing; even between speakers of the same language we cannot say what we mean. Eros and language, intercourse and discourse, are inextricably connected and represent the most intimate and most dangerous forms of human communication. We never know in either case—making love or making sense—whether what we feel or intend is being felt or understood. That eros and language have common roots in our deepest and most mythic selves is suggested by our complex of taboos and rituals, forbidden words and forbidden parts of the body and forbidden acts of sex, and the ritual importance of acts of language and acts of sex and, as George Steiner reminded us, the apparent relation between sexual perversions and incorrect speech.

And there is much more than this to understand about language. If we think of the uses of speech and the manipulation of populations, of its use as a tool of tyrants, we understand that no student of language is a student of language only. We understand that to study language is to study all that we are or ever have been. The prerequisite act of translation is to know the culture that produced the original work and the psychology of which its language is a part.

And so we must understand that we cannot talk seriously of translation without shedding, however painfully, our linguistic chauvinism. There are between four thousand and five thousand languages in current use. Each year so-called rare languages, tongues spoken by isolated or moribund ethnic communities, become extinct, and some of the languages now dead are among the splendors of human intelligence. Today entire families of language survive only in the uncertain remembrance of the old or in the limbo of tape recordings. At almost every moment some ancient and rich expression lapses irretrievably into silence.

With translation, as with original work, we must honor the language and the idea of language, be of honest mind and have a professional attitude, and we must not be lazy. Even then we will not succeed as we mean to, but there is a kind of success in getting closer to the original work than we thought we would, in paying an honest homage to another writer, and in saying to other readers, "Look, here's somebody I want you to know about."

As *translation* means a "carrying across," the act of translation is a bridge that carries a literary work from one language to another. At its best it is a bridge the original author seems to cross to speak our own language to us. The job of the translator is to build the bridge well. The fact of it is—the joy of it is—that it's a hard bridge to build.

What we mostly hope for, those of us who practice this sweet and terrible craft, is not to be one of those described by John Nims in his lengthy four-line poem called "Verse Translator":

> Goethe, Racine, Neruda, Pushkin—next!
> Some Choctaw? Aztec epic? Or Czech text?
> Lo at his touch as he invades *tromp, tromp*
> Mountain on mountain, groaning, turns to swamp.

The Writer in the World

Let Me Not to the Marriage of True Minds
The Writer on Campus

$\mathcal{F}$irst off, we can't speak of "the writer" as if it were a collective intelligence. For that matter, there is no such thing as "the campus" either. There are writers, and there are campuses, and we have to be careful not to think of them as if either were simply a multinucleated amoeba held together by some invisible and mystic plasm. Still, there are some things to be said about most writers, most campuses without graduate writing programs, and most students. While I have an aversion to generalizations, I'm going to grit my teeth and make some about the relationship of all three, in the interest of all three.

The writer generally comes to the campus to earn more than his writing alone will afford him, to enjoy the contacts found there, and for the joy of teaching—one or more of these things. But let's assume that being on a faculty, the writer is performing in a manner satisfactory to a department head or wouldn't be there. So we don't need to concern ourselves with the writer's obligations to the college. Maybe I'm showing a prejudice, but I've never known a writer on a college faculty who was not trying very hard to write and publish, to guide students who wanted to write and publish, and to teach well what courses were assigned. What I'm concerned with here is the attitude of the college toward the writer and toward the role the writer ought to play as a part of that college. I feel sure that this attitude differs little from campus to campus, and that it isn't a happy one for the writer, for the faculty, or for the students, since it tends to make difficult, if not downright impossible, the very job the writer is there to do. Whatever a writer on campus may want to be to the students and to his fellow faculty members, there is going to be more frustration than fulfillment unless that writer shares the image of "the writer on campus" that colleagues have built in their fancies.

What is that image? Well, if we could throw the nerves of a thousand associate professors on a screen, we would get a pattern something like this: The writer is first of all an ornament on the campus, a colorful afterthought, a decoration on the academic tree. Exactly where that ornament hangs is difficult to say; it is certainly not the star, but it's not so much sub-academic as para-academic—out on a limb, as it were.

The "scholar," one who writes about what creative writers have written, generally carries in a vest pocket of the mind an English-academic dictionary that defines *scholar* and *writer* in terms of a curious juxtaposition, to the disadvantage of the creative writer. There is the belief abroad, for instance, that scholarship somehow comes first in the order of things. Now, I know, of course, that for the student who has no intention of becoming a writer, explication and discussion of a text is a sensible means of teaching about literature, and the scholar is perfectly competent to do this. But it does not follow that because the classroom teacher acts as at least an elementary kind of critic, that because our study of a creative work often begins with criticism, scholarship is therefore the root of literature. We go too far when we imply to students that the purpose in writing a poem is to get it criticized. There are academics who look on the creative writer with such scorn as this and who must, to be consistent, consider football the invention of sports writers.

There is the suspicion that writing a poem or a story will even nullify scholarly credentials. A friend of mine who, besides publishing a novel and four books of poems, had earned his DPhil from a British university was recently offered a position on a well-known southern campus. When he asked what classes he would have, he was given to understand that he wouldn't "have to" teach heavy courses, that since he was a writer he would have only the survey and creative writing. He was answered with raised eyebrows and a confused silence when he reminded the department head and the committee that he was a scholar, with the degrees, critical articles, and footnotes to prove it, and that he certainly would expect an advanced course in his field. Then, after the silence: "But you *are* a *writer?*"

We leap from this to the conviction that the doctorate, which means nothing if you are a writer, is the be-all and end-all if you want to be a scholar or teach courses with meat on them and is the final measure of one's worth as a teacher or as a scholar. One department head was recently heard to say that he didn't think he'd be interested in anyone without academic credentials. What he meant by that, I think, was that he wanted the PhD as proof that a person was qualified to do scholarly work and would prefer this to the scholarly work itself, with or without the PhD, as proof.

Lest I be accused of defending my own lack of education, let me point out that more than a few writers of important scholarship either have lacked it also or have indicated rather convincingly that formal classroom work, if a helpful supplement to self-discipline and drive, was not the sine qua non of learning. Here, as a matter of interest, are some of those scholars who have stumbled along with out the Union Card: T. S. Eliot,

John Crowe Ransom, Allen Tate, Robert Penn Warren, Donald Davidson, John Ciardi, James Dickey, I. A. Richards, Cleanth Brooks, William Empson, R. P. Blackmur, and others.

This indicates, I think, that one might enter into the realms of the don by one's own ladder and even that we are more likely to see a creative writer venture into scholarship than a scholar venture into the writing of poems and stories, which also says something about the order of things, and about the importance attached to the chair of creative writing on any campus.

I know that some schools may want a writer in the catalog but not on campus, that there is no thought of the school as patron or even as partner, but as recipient of the writer's name and good offices, and all the prestige and vainglory clinging to them.

Well, what of it? If this view of the writer's role is a common one, as I believe it is, so what? Does the writer have any business on the faculty in the first place?

As much, I guess, as the painter or sculptor in the art department or the composer in the music department. The university stands to gain a great deal from the relationship, when the writer is writing and talking as a practicing writer to the students. Or to colleagues, for that matter. The truth is that an English department has no business being without a writer. We have to remind ourselves again that English scholarship was invented as an instrument of study, that it depends upon and serves the object of that study, namely, the thing written. Writing does not feed on criticism or on the classroom, but criticism and the classroom necessarily feed on writing; they can't live without it.

It seems logical that the closer contact students (and faculty) have with the act of making a poem or a story, the more they listen to a writer talk about writing, the more opportunities they have to take part in a writer-reader dialogue, the more intelligent will be the act of criticism.

When criticism rises out of a critic's monologue, or at best out of a dialogue between critic and critic, especially when the subject is contemporary literature, the critic is being unfair to readers, and to the work at hand. There are two sides to any work of literature: the writer's and the reader's. Our reading is richer—and especially richer is the act of reading over our own shoulder, what we call criticism—when we have some understanding of where the thing written came from and how it came to be.

Then on every campus are those students who want to write, who are, or who believe themselves to be, poets and storytellers. They ask for criticism of a finished work, and they can get it easily enough from any astute, honest, and mature reader around. But if they want criticism of work in progress? If they have a poem undone or overdone? What then? The usual critic, the scholar who is not a writer, is as lost here as most sports writers would be if they were dropped onto a football field in the middle of a game.

So much for the school, for the young writers, the young critics, and those who simply want to learn to read. If we can agree that maybe they can profit from the writer's presence, there is still the writer to think of. What about all those writers who we hear have been lost in the Groves of Academe, never to be seen again? What about all those writers who have been undone by the classroom and the campus? Well, I don't believe it. There are some things, I suppose, that can ruin a good writer, but the campus is not one of them, except as it takes a person's time; neither, for that matter, is Wall Street or Madison Avenue or the wrapping counter at Zebo's Butcher Shop. Eight hours a day in one of these places probably won't make a person write any better; they assuredly will not make one's writing worse. I have spent my time hitchhiking across the country and sharing a cruddy pad, and I have spent my time managing a Sears, Roebuck furniture department. My writing was no worse at one time than the other. I like to think it would take more than that kind of change in my environment to strike me dumb. I like to think I carry a good part of my environment with me. Any writer who doesn't had better be able to sell furniture, and any writer who can be destroyed by a university didn't have much to destroy in the first place.

Is there any reason, then, why this marriage should not take place? Not if both parties know what they're getting into—if the writer is not simply looking for a sinecure, and if the school is not looking for decoration. There may be writers who have settled into an English department because it's a soft job and nobody expects anything of them, neither the administration nor the students. There may be, but I don't know them. What I do know are any number of schools who have weighed writers down with a full load of courses. Let's take a walk with C. P. Snow to the other side of the campus. Try to imagine a young chemist doing respectable research and publishing in the right journals at reasonable intervals. That's called "producing." It would be difficult to find such a person at less than the associate-professor level, without a research assistant, and without all the necessary equipment and supplies.

What about the writer on the same campus, who is also "producing," publishing poetry and/or fiction regularly and respectably? I have recently corresponded or spoken directly with more than twenty writers-on-campus around the country and have had confirmed my belief that the setup is generally unsatisfactory. At a typewriter instead of an analytical balance, this same "productive" person can be very easily found as an instructor, teaching as many as twelve hours (of which as many as six may be composition courses), without a typist or a student grader.

But the writer stays because it still beats selling shoes. Probably. But it should do more than just beat selling shoes; the shoe store has nothing much to gain from the association and so has little reason to put much into it. When a university makes it difficult for a writer to work, not only is the university losing bibliography but the students are losing the writer's advice and criticism, which, apart from some doubtful prestige, is the only return the school can, or should, expect from its investment in a writer.

Beyond this, there are several areas in which the college and the writer can serve each other. The campus offers an excellent forum for literary head-knocking, and a publishing writer with a knowledge of who is what in the writing world, of who digs and what cuts, with the friendships with other writers, with a grasp of contemporary—I mean to say current—work of interest and probably of significance, should certainly be available to the school for counsel to whatever committees invite readers and plan literary forums. The administration of a school should not allow such a committee to function without that counsel, or let a journal featuring poetry and fiction operate without the guidance (at least) of any reputable poet or fiction writer around. I have known this to happen too, though, which is as sensible as having a conference on space flight run by mathematicians and not a veteran astronaut in attendance.

Dear Writer,
    This is an invitation to become a member of our faculty

this fall as Writer-in-Residence, at a beginning salary of enough.

Since we are aware that science is handmaiden to the arts, and since the handmaiden has already got hers, we are, in the interest of the order of things, offering you also a six-hour load, freedom from composition courses, together with typing help and an office typewriter.

Sincerely, no kidding,

The Dean

Dear Dean,

Thank you for the invitation. I will be very happy to join your faculty, read the students' writing and criticize it, join in seminars, talk to college and town literary-and-otherwise clubs, help in the editing of the University Review, offer any services in the planning of lyceum programs, and please the board of trustees with my annual list of publications.

Your offer is goodly, Sire, and I would not ask for anything more after paper, postage stamps, and a key to my door.

Sincerely also,

Writer

And they lived happily ever after? More or less. Anyway, they stay together—and I suspect they ought to—for much the same reason any pair stay together: for appearances, for economic reasons, for the children, and because, sometimes, they like each other.

The Writer and the Editor

> The relationship between author and copy editor is not
> always smooth, but if one's best friend is not inclined to
> be one's hardest reader, then the hardest reader had best
> be seen as a friend.

*T*here is, however much we might wish it otherwise, a kind
of adversary relationship between author and publisher. Both
want their books published, but not for quite the same reasons
nor in the same way. The publisher wants a conventional style;
the author wants an unconventional style. The publisher wants
to sell the book for as much as the market will pay; the author
wants the book to sell at cost. The publisher wants co-op advertising; the author wants a full page in the *New York Times.*
The publisher wants to print fifteen hundred; the author wants
fifteen thousand. The publisher wants half of all movie, TV, and
reprint rights; the author wants it all.

Let me admit right off that my own views on this subject
have moderated somewhat over the years, mostly because of my
years as director of a university press. It's remarkable how such a
move can clarify one's vision. Still, when I'm in the role of writer
I do think as one, and then I see the publisher as partner in a not
wholly comfortable symbiotic relationship; when I was in the
role of publisher, it was sometimes hard for me to understand
how authors could be as difficult as they were. The change is
similar to what happens when a driver parks the car and walks
across the street: there is suddenly common cause with those
pedestrians who a moment before were so irritating, and common suspicion toward anyone behind a wheel.

Most conflicts between author and publisher arise over options and other secondary rights; when a book should be allowed to go out of print; and the relationship between author and manuscript editor. My comments are directed only to the third of these because it is at the same time the most worrisome and the most easily addressed. It is the most worrisome because the manuscript editor is the only person at a press with whom most authors have substantial contact. To many writers, in fact, the personality and character of the press are precisely those of the manuscript editor.

It may help us to understand the author's view if, like the author, we see the editor as a critic. The reviewing critic says in public what a work should have been; the editor-critic says in private what it ought to become. Both make it their business to second-guess the author, and no one, however big he or she tries to be about it, likes to be second-guessed. So critics of both types are bound to meet resistance in the author's mind. The judgments of the reviewing critic, even though they are public, are often the less disturbing because there are other such critics, perhaps kinder ones, yet to be heard from. There is, alas, only one editor.

The young writer's first defense against either is the old and easy question, If she knows so much about writing, why is she working on my book instead of her own? This is specious, of course. For one thing, some editors are indeed writers. Most important, one can know very well the adjustments an expert needs to make in order to improve without being as skilled as the expert. If this were not so, Muhammad Ali would not have had a trainer, nor Van Cliburn a music coach.

It is specious also because the very critic a writer needs before a work sees print is one who can represent, not other writers, but the literate and objective reader who is not a professional author.

I recently heard a young writer say that every author ought to have a detached ear. The image may be discomfiting, but the admonition is valid. That's what a good editor is. If one's best friend is not inclined to be one's hardest reader, then the hardest reader had best be seen as a friend. I have been saved by such friends more than once. I am not the only author to feel grateful for that redeeming attention. A warm letter of acknowledgment to the person with the blue pencil—or what used to be a blue pencil—is no rarity.

So why do we have so much trouble? Why do authors speak of their editors often in uncomplimentary terms, especially while a manuscript is in press?

From the editor's standpoint the answer is simple. The problem is the author's ego, an insecure and inflated ego that cannot allow for suggestions of imperfection in style or content. From the author's standpoint the answer is also simple. The problem is the editor's ego, the need to feel important by changing what the editor's mind could not originate and by forcing a creative spirit into a mold. We should probably occasionally give some credence to both charges, but I don't believe that most authors or most editors are well described by either of them. I suspect that most authors and most editors mean to do what they do as well as they can do it and know that each needs the other for a book to happen. The problem, I suggest, is almost wholly one of style.

Since the editor makes the first personal contact, it is usually the editor who sets the style. Unfortunately, what is intended to be a preliminary salve often lands as an opening salvo in a battle of hurt feelings and misunderstanding. Two letters from the editor usually come to the writer's desk, one announcing that this editor has been given the responsibility of working on this writer's manuscript and a later one accompanying the manuscript after it has been edited. The letters sometimes are irritating—never by design, certainly—and often they make the author uneasy about what's going to happen to the work. The feeling is not very different from that of a parent watching a child taken down a hospital corridor where mother and father may not follow.

A number of apparently innocuous moves can get the relationship off to a bad start. It is presumptuous and perilous to assume that an author wants to be addressed by first name. Many initial editorial letters begin with something like: "Dear Mary (may we start out on a first-name basis?)." This puts Mary in a position of either accepting this or seeming rude herself. "No, we may not!" is about the only negative response available.

I saw one first letter to an author named Gustav Mullen with the greeting "Dear Gus." It seems to me that it would be better, and just as easy, to open the initial letter "Dear Professor Mullen," and close with the typed "Sincerely, John Jackson, Editor," signed simply "John" with a handwritten postscript saying, "We're going to be working together pretty closely over the next few months, and I would feel more comfortable being on a first-name basis, if this is all right with you. In any case, I will follow your wishes." With rare exceptions, I think, Professor Mullen will write back "Dear John" and sign himself "Gustav" or even "Gus." If not, this approach allows the author simply to ignore the note and continue on a more formal basis. Alternatively, the first-name basis may be allowed to develop naturally over time.

Sometimes, as well, the tone of the editor's letter is patronizing. Here are actual lines from two examples. First, "I have made minor changes in capitalization, punctuation, and hyphenation to bring the manuscript into conformity with style used at this Press. The high quality of your writing left me little else to do, though there were some cases where I felt some rewriting was necessary for maximum clarity." This accompanied a completely rewritten manuscript in which, for instance, "the poet's career" became "the corpus of the poet's work," and "even though" became "notwithstanding the fact that." It was obvious from the condition of the manuscript that the editor did not consider the writing to be of high quality.

And this: "I have also done some rewriting of unclear or awkward passages in order to bring your writing up to its highest potential." What writer could respond warmly to that? In the touch-and-run relationships of most authors and their editors the editor can hope, at most, to be accepted as a representative of the reader the author is hoping for.

Surely it would be better, and just as simple, to say to the author something like this: "I've tried to read your manuscript as if I were that literate and interested reader we believe it will find, and to catch any turns of phrase or passages that seem unclear or out of tone (and of course any technical slips in spelling, syntax, and so forth). I hope you will feel that a second pair of eyes has been useful to you. I admire your work."

I don't know a writer whose resistance to editing would not be considerably eroded by that approach. For one thing, it avoids the word *rewritten,* an awful word for a writer. For another, it avoids the suggestion that in the phrases *house style* and *writer's style* the word *style* means the same thing. Certainly it does not, and the implication that it does, and especially that the house style is the right one, is bound to be galling to a writer. For a third, it avoids the assumption that the editor's changes make the manuscript better in any absolute way; they simply say to the author, "You're an excellent writer; I'm an excellent reader.

My job is to represent your reader to you, and tell you when that reader is likely to be jolted or confused." All this will work better, of course, if the editor actually has read the manuscript before writing the first letter.

Also, the author will have more faith in the editor's skill and wisdom if much is not made of narrow distinctions. Persistent hairsplitting is as destructive to this partnership as it is to any other. I know one novelist who found that in his novel set in nineteenth-century England the officers' *sabres* had all been changed to *sabers.* He was not pleased.

I feel, as I believe most authors do, that many manuscript editors make much too much of the distinction between *which* and *that* in nonrestrictive clauses. It's an affliction peculiar to the trade, but I think it will pass in time. The *Chicago Manual* is sometimes called "the editor's bible." I submit that the mature and confident editor might better take C. S. Lewis's approach to that book and not Jerry Falwell's.

Walt Disney found in the early days of his work in animation that by giving his characters only three fingers on each hand he could save enough money in time and ink over a remarkably short time to do an additional cartoon. Think what might be saved by a publisher if, on a hundred books a year, all the editors paid attention only to what truly would confuse or jolt a good reader or embarrass the writer or the press.

I will admit that if this were done, we would lose some of the marvelous stories we now have to tell at conferences. For example, about the copy editor of an anthology who changed *which* to *that* and *that* to *which* in included works by William Styron and Thornton Wilder. Or about the anguish of the poet John Ciardi during the production of a book of poems in which he referred satirically to *Untied Airlines.* In the edited manuscript it was changed, of course, to *United Airlines.* He changed it back and wrote "stet" above it. It returned in galleys as *United Airlines.* Then again in page proof. Each time he changed it back. It appeared in the book as *United Airlines.*

Let me include here a note of love and thanks to an editor who kept me from appearing a fool before the world. One of my poems has the speaker sitting in a studio watching a square of light, formed by the sunlight coming through a window behind him, creep up the wall as the sun sets. The poem began, "The window here is hung in the east wall." A number of friends had read the poem and seemed to like it and said nothing else. It took an editor to ask me where I found the sun setting in the east. To say that I am grateful is to say too little.

I have known authors to send flowers to their editors. Candy. Theater tickets. One I know sent an airline ticket from the editor's city to his, not only because of what the editor had done but because of the gracious and professional way in which she had done it.

A friend of mine thirty years ago corrected this marvelous typographical error: "Life is so short, we must make the most of every minuet." It hurt him to make that change as much as authors may be pained by the work of editors. Yet writers will suffer in peace, and even gladly, if they can believe that only those changes are made that should be made and if those necessary changes are made with sensitivity and in a context of common sense.

Poetry and the Place of Place

$\mathcal{A}$ good poem is made only in small part by the one who holds the pen and in great part by the ghosts that live in the writer's house. I'm a southern writer because I'm a writer and a southerner, and I feel sorry for any writer, especially of poetry or fiction, whose title doesn't have a place attached to it.

What matters is not to be a southern writer but to have people and a geography. Certainly a writer who is a southerner lives in a world different from the world of writers who are not, but so does the writer from the southwest live in a special world, and a writer from New England. A poet from Wales is not going to make the same poetry as one from Ireland. This is not to place a judgment on the poems but to recognize the role of the past, like DNA of the spirit, the sense of a land, and of its people, that gives a work much of the quality we call style.

The imprint of geography and geology, weather, and the pace of life makes such writing not only distinctive from but also better than writing with little sign of where it came from. The wrinkles, folds, and scratches caused by a land and those who live on it enrich a reader's experience, sharpening the reader's feeling of having been somewhere and found something.

The existence of recognizable regions, each even now with its own way of going, is not what causes trouble between peoples. Trouble lies in the lack of respect for those differences. Respect doesn't grow out of a pretended homogeneity; it comes with an understanding and acceptance and finally a celebration of the ways we differ. If we were in fact all of one color and of one faith, speaking the same language with the same accent, there would not be more love in the world, and there would be no less hate. But it would be a sad thing to travel from New Orleans to Honolulu to Seattle to New York without noticing that one had left New Orleans, to travel without going anywhere. To say that one wants to be a writer and then to write with no sense of the people and places, the history and myth, one came out of is the same as saying that one's way of walking and loving, joking and dying, can escape being shaped by the woman and man one came from and the houses one walked by on the way to school.

The southerner may have a greater awareness of region and roots than many Americans do, but there are others who feel it just as strongly. The American Jew, without a defined place on this continent, has a keen sense of roots. It may not be coincidence that so much of this country's good writing has been done by southerners and Jews. Or that the African American became a much more important presence in our literature as the black writer became aware of and jealous of those very differences that make for blackness and hearken back to the history of a people and a way of being in the world. Writers like Gerald Barrax and Ernest Gaines and Brenda Marie Osbey, James Alan Mcpherson and Al Aubert, Alice Walker and Marilyn Nelson and Al Young, all both black and southern, are richer in this than most of us, and their writing shows it.

The Scientist and the Humanist

Some Observations on a Misunderstanding between Us and Why It Matters

The following essay had its beginnings in a long and fragmented dialogue between John William Corrington and me during our days together at Louisiana State University. The sciences and the humanities were mutually exclusive and inimical, we wrote together and separately, intercalating paragraphs and editing each other's sentences, until after a while we were not sure which of us had written what. The first two-thirds or so of the essay grew in that way. For the final pages I take full responsibility, but I think Bill would have said that he wanted to share in it.

I may as well tell you, to begin with, that before I'm through I am going to address myself, not to the various real and fancied differences between us, but to our ultimate kinship. I want to describe that common base on which all human pursuit rests and in terms of which the scientist and the humanist, the economist and the philosopher, the publisher and the banker not only can but must build together.

But "Ah," the practical mind says, "How can that be? The world of some—of the poet, the painter, the dancer—is not even a real world. It is a world of illusion."

There is a story of a man riding on a train with a large box in his lap. The box had what appeared to be air holes in it, and from time to time the man would raise the lid very slightly and look inside.

A traveler sitting across the aisle from the man had been watching him for a long time, wondering what was in the box, what the man could be transporting in his lap with such care. Finally, when he was not able to contain himself any longer, he leaned across and said, "Hey, fella, what you got in that box?"

The man looked for a moment as if he didn't want to give away his secret. Then finally he said, "A mongoose. I got a mongoose in here."

"Oh," the second man said. "Well, uh . . . what you gonna do with a mongoose?"

"It's for my brother. He's an alcoholic."

"An *alcoholic!*"

"Yeah. Well, you see, when he drinks he sees snakes. Thousands of snakes. They scare him to death. Now he can let the mongoose out and it'll eat them."

"Aw, come on," the man said. "Those are not real snakes."

"That's all right, " the man with the box said, lifting the lid and peeking inside again, with a look of deep satisfaction on his face. "It's not a real mongoose."

The scientist is right. The world of the poet is not a real world. But that's all right. Neither is the world of the scientist. That is, if by real we mean that world in which what we see is what is there. That world in which our senses tell us what is true and common sense is something to be believed.

Our senses told us that the sun went around the earth, that a road grew narrow as it ran into the distance. Common sense tells us that if we have flipped ten heads in a row, the chances of flipping tails on the eleventh try are thereby enhanced. Our senses tell us that a table is solid, and our common sense tells us that a large stone should fall faster than a small one.

What is the real world? Let's say that the world of what we think of as hard and usable knowledge and the world of the humanities are *important* worlds, worlds we choose to build and to live in. The question is whether, having done this, we are doomed to live in these two worlds, out of sight of one another, with no lines of communication between us, no memory of our common origins, no sense of that union—or perhaps that confederacy—that must hold us as people ultimately if loosely together.

This is the question I want to deal with. But let me go back a way and work up to it, taking science to represent all the pursuits of and use of hard facts, as it was at first the whole body of those facts. Or what were believed to be facts. Let me use the artist to represent the pursuit of imaginary ends and impractical insights, soft knowledge if knowledge at all.

The science of the Greeks dealt with generalities, teleologies, myths; the rebirth of science, with such observers as Copernicus, concerned itself at first with particulars, the special behavior of water, planets, the uses of numbers. Slowly the single discoveries were seen to form a system, and from the system were extrapolated principles, laws.

Science still works *in the laboratory* with tangibles, in a wise concession to its own limitations, in a sometimes reluctant homage to that thing called the scientific method, which decrees that all principles will be arrived at by carefully observed and controlled application of that method.

Science, though, is not finally interested in the thing itself; it moves as soon as it can away from a particular to $F = ma$, $E = mc^2$, that the pressure exerted by a contained gas varies inversely with volume and directly with temperature. It moves from the sentence to the equation, from the word to the number.

The very quality of mystery and ambiguity, those fugitive causes that reside in words and make them the vehicle of our most deeply felt and cherished values, renders words unfit for the use of science. The lack of human accretions, of emotion, of memories, of marvelous and terrible associations, renders the mathematical symbol ideal for the purely conceptual work of science.

Now, the truth is that math and all other instruments and techniques are used by a scientist to pull away from the human condition. Insofar as one is a creature of love and hate, of fear and self-delusion and maniacal certainties, one cannot hope to serve science. Only by escaping the endless contradictions and confusions of the purely human world, the world of poetry and pride, of sidewalk preaching and used-car dealers—all using the small language of words—only by setting aside these things can the scientist hope to deal with the phenomenological universe.

The artist, on the other hand, and by this I mean the person who creates for us an illusion of natural experience in which we can participate, is less concerned with concept. The artist works with details, with particular things, with the furniture of this world, in order to stir our imaginations to a sense of experience, half vicarious, half empirical. The artist is content to let others arrive at any "truth" by means of that experience. The poem is a thing, built of particularities, and insomuch as it loses its very particularity it loses its value as a poem. We are told, anyway, that this points to a difference, a significant difference, between the scientist and the humanist. But is it?

We sometimes think of the scientist as deductive, moving by way of the general—the principle—which is supposed to be the bailiwick of the scientist—to the specific, the application, to vaccines and motor oil. We say that the poet is inductive, starting with the particular and from that drawing the idea. But here we are confusing scientist with engineer, which is the habit of our culture.

It's a bad habit, and it ought to be broken. The scientist *be-*

gins with particulars, in fact or in fancy, and from the nature of these particulars extrapolates principles; the engineer employs these principles to build a bridge or a rocket and so comes back full circle to the particular. But if we are to speak of the two fields as one, then we can say that science in the broadest sense watches the thing, figures out what general rules are directing it, causing it to behave in a certain way, and employs these same rules to be able to (1) anticipate behavior and (2) control it.

The humanist—the philosopher, the theologian, the historian—also studies the thing, which is the human being, and tries to figure out what makes us act as we do, whether there is a system working through our comings and our goings.

So what is the difference, then? Are we to conclude that there is none? Let's look again. We can say that the scientist *as* scientist is concerned with hard knowledge and *as* engineer is concerned with its utility, so that broadly the concern with science and technology is with the discovery and application of principles to predict and control the behavior of nature. The humanist, on the other hand, is concerned with the *value* of *communications* of an experience, with what meaning or insight is to be drawn from it. This is the dichotomy spoken of in the admonition "With all thy knowledge, get understanding." It is the dichotomy to which Adlai Stevenson referred when he cautioned us that we not let our know *how* too far ahead of our know *why.* And this is the dichotomy we have generally come to accept, to believe is fair. We have let ourselves rest here. But if we examine it more closely, we may see that we have to redefine *science,* and even *knowing,* which of course is what *science* means; that some, perhaps all, of the principles we have called "scientific" may be more universal than the word implies.

History began with the telling of stories from the past, then from it came sociology, the observation of myths in the making. History had become a running commentary, and the sociologist, extracting from that commentary, began formulating principles of human behavior: $F = ma$; it's harder to get a hundred people to shut up than three. When a force is applied to an equation in equilibrium, the equation shifts to satisfy the force, and then a new equilibrium is established; when a traditional relationship between two races or two genders is subjected to a force in favor of one, the relationship shifts to satisfy the new force, and ultimately a new relationship is established. And then the sociologist begins predicting, and even, by means of city planning and antipoverty programs, controlling.

It is at this point, by these acts, that sociology becomes social science. The distinction has blurred again. And when the poet *manipulates* the *devices* of the poem in order to move us, stir our imaginations, and excite the consciousness because the poet knows what combinations of sound and meaning will serve those ends, are we to say that the poet is a scientist? Perhaps, anyway, an engineer of language?

Let us dwell on the sum total of things and say that the practical mind is concerned *primarily* with *the way* nature works, and the humanist, generally and first, asks *to what end* nature works. Humanism, we like to say, is concerned with value, ethical and aesthetic. But even so, are these concerns mutually exclusive and inimical? Certainly not to the mind of the person as a person. No poet would want a world of isolated particulars, and in fact by means of the metaphor the poet tries to tie them together out of that apparent isolation. And what physical scientist—or philosopher or economist—would ask for a world of active principles only, without a particular pair of shoes, a particular fountain pen, a particular woman or man?

George Santayana has given both worlds the nod in two luminous pronouncements. He admonishes those of us who love "science" too much, who might be inclined to turn everything into a grotesque kind of science, who would make our subjective and sensory selves, our religion and our poetry, second to that attitude we call scientific: "Mythology cannot become science by being reduced in bulk, but it may cease, as a mythology, to be worth having." To those who love science too little, who are afraid that science will destroy art, literature, and religion, he says: "The growth of what is known increases the scope of what may be imagined and hoped for." And so he begins to bind us together.

There are honest people in the humanities with hostility toward the sciences—real fears, objections that demand answers. These objections fall roughly into five categories: the ontological, the romantic, the classical, the personal, and the religious.

By the ontological objection we mean the feeling that science ignores, even degrades, the thing in itself in favor of the class, the generic. This is the defense of the sensual, the stuff of experience and ultimate knowledge. This objection, of course, could as well be directed toward philosophy, for the philosopher has always been the natural ally of the scientist, not of the poet—as Plato made clear. And those making the objection in favor of the thing in itself against the general, the treatment of things as a class, find as their natural allies not only the poets and painters but the makers of automobiles and breakfast cereals, of television commercials and billboards.

The romantic objection is the defense of the part of us that, again in the words of Santayana, "aches for new conquests of new fictions." As a species, we long for our past, for freedom and magic, for adventure, for glory. We are afraid at times that cold fact, practicality, and the melting away of mystery will leave us hungry for things we will find were not expendable.

The classical objection comes from those who want the apparently clear and unambiguous simplicity of Platonic or Aristotelian thought and feel that modern science, in spite of Heisenberg, clutters and complicates, makes the world complex when it should not be.

The personal objection says, "I am important. I am significant. I have value that our microscopes and scales can't measure. I have an ego. I am one person, and the center of a very real universe. You ignore me."

The religious objection is very close to this, of course. It says, "The person is important, as a creature of God, and outside God there is neither value nor meaning. You ignore God." This is the objection we hear most often in arguments about origins, teleology, and final causes, in arguments about creationism, and faith healing.

To all these—and to the scientist—my answer is this: we are talking about the wrong things. This is what I have been saying, and what I have been doing. One simple idea engulfs all of us if we are truly human. That idea is what I'm setting forth: that the chemist, the poet, the painter, the economist, the sociologist, the taxi dispatcher, the legislator, the theologian, the taxonomist, the mathematician, and the musician are concerned with one thing in the last analysis. They are concerned with order. For it is in order that we find beauty, predictability, and perhaps God. Order is our abiding concern, the thing we most want to find in nature and to create. Order is a synonym for value, the stuff of mathematics, the secret of what we call beauty, the framework of experimental science, and the only problem of philosophy. The new discoveries in the study of chaos and the formulations of chaos theory do not lessen our hunger for order or say that the universe is not acting in an orderly fashion. It says that the order of the universe is more complex than we thought it was.

In the face of chaos theory it is not less true that in large measure our intellect (that is, our conceptual consciousness) and our spirit (a harder thing to define; shall we define it as the capacity to reach out beyond ourselves and all phenomena toward eternity, transcendence?) are the products of, and dependent upon, our ability to *structure* reality, our capacity to bind together the most disparate elements of our experience within the symbol systems that we have created in the past and that we continue to generate.

Notice the implications of this. If we are unique in that we are symbol-making creatures, to what *end* do we construct mathematical systems? To what end have we been both creator and servant of myths of creation and fall, resurrection and transfiguration? Why do we write and paint and shape stone, classify flora and fauna, organize the stars and the strata of earth into patterns and systems? The answer, I believe, is comparatively simple, but it is the best part of knowledge: the human soul, however we choose to define that word, is possessed with a rage for order. It's very unfortunate that *order* has been used in unsavory ways over the last decades, in Hitler's New Order, Nixon's Law and Order, and the first Bush's New World Order, and for even longer in the "The class will come to order," "Order in the court."

I'm using *order* here to mean the network of natural connections between individuals in a community. Order. The sense of order. Art. Science. Politics. Religion. Sociology. Marketing and distribution. Education. The need to see things in their proper relationships. The need to find in chaos the patterns that hide there, to find those forms within ourselves as well as to find ourselves within the forms.

I recall an exchange that may help to illustrate how the hard scientist and the politician, the psychologist and the poet, all pursuits and all people, share this understanding. It is said that astronomically speaking, the human being is only a speck of dust on a tiny planet in the outer reaches of a minor galaxy. It has been answered that astronomically speaking, the human being *is the astronomer.*

Astronomy and physics and chemistry aside, the great study, the eternal study, the study we too often put aside, much to our cost, is of the human being, for finally the astronomer is a human being. The physicist is a human being. The chemist is a human being. We are born human, and whatever we become in between, it is as humans that we take leave of the phenomenological world.

So I speak of order and of the human mind. The link is the human spirit. A fiction? Fair enough. Niels Bohr's atom was also a fiction. But it worked, for a while. We know more because of our use of that model. And who is to say that quarks and mesons are not fictions now, to be replaced by more sophisticated fictions as we need them? Every symbol is a kind of fiction, and everything we know through cognition is a symbol.

We never truly experience an affectionate dog or dinnertime or a walk in the woods as a thing in itself. Only a mindless creature can experience raw phenomena. As soon as our senses perceive an object, our minds cast over it the mysterious cloak of symbolic representation. The object is informed by all we have ever experienced. We cannot walk in the woods or on a beach without the memory of similar walks rising to go with us. In short, as adults we cannot have a discreet experience. The experience itself becomes a symbol, and so a kind of fiction.

It is the supreme fictions created by the human spirit that give all value, all purpose, to our lives. We are biologists and dancers because we wish to know the world and to put the world in order. We are poets and economists for the same reason. And we erect mathematical systems and multitudinous classifications in order to shape and contain our knowing.

So we discover myths to structure our inner life as mathematics structures the world outside. Always we come back to the human spirit seeking to order the universe in which it exists. One symbol serves to clarify another. We destroy one symbol to shape a better one. The result is an expansion of order: things become intelligible.

Confusion, outside us and within, is stayed or passed through, and the area in which we not only survive but grow and fulfill our potential becomes wider. Order is the charmed circle within which the human dominion is made secure. Beyond order lies that dark confusion filled with endless storms of nullity into which we venture at our peril.

The darkness and the confusion are both macrocosmic and microcosmic. There is confusion to be ordered where astronauts venture today, but there is confusion, too, in the minds of people who are held hostage by schizophrenia. The absence of our own human order in deep space could not be more frightening than the chaos in the mind of Lee Harvey Oswald one November day.

In our time, with the ghosts of Aristotle and of Newton, of Curie and Planck and Heraclitus, beside us, we are embarked on the voyage of discovery that we have dreamed of since first we saw the orderly procession of stars through the night sky.

We will go out now to those stars and into the tiniest particle our instruments and theories can identify. But we will go as humans, with a history and a politics, with a theology and a philosophy. We will go with a literature that contains them all. We will go, all of us, in our common purpose to find order, or we will find that the trip is purposeless and that nothing we may discover can compensate for what we have lost.

If the need for order and the endless search for order are a bond between the scientist and the humanist, the new realizations of science that continually challenge our sense of order bind us even closer. We learn through quantum mechanics that electrons—of which we are built—may have no material substance. And apart from quantum mechanics itself, much of contemporary science raises questions about the nature of reality. Some of these grow out of the concept of relativity, which Einstein tried unsuccessfully to divorce from quantum mechanics.

Looking at the universe in the context of relativity, we can see—without theorems or mathematics—how questionable our sense of time and space is. Imagine that all matter in the universe is compressed into a single ball, now the only object in existence. Imagine it moving.

No matter where it "moves," while it remains the center of all mass, it remains at the center of the universe; if it cannot leave that center, it cannot move. Movement can exist, then, only when at least two objects exist, which means that movement is not absolute but a function of the interaction between objects; if space is recognized as the distance between objects and time as what transpires when space is traversed, time and space are also seen as functions of movement and of the relationships between objects, and not as absolutes in themselves.

Chaos theory argues persuasively that the sort of order we perceive in the universe is not universal but local. Quantum mechanics and the growing scientific discussion surrounding it raise a great many such questions about the nature of reality; volumes and centuries will be required to wrestle with all of them.

Questions of a religious nature, though, will most insistently demand reexamination. This is because matters of religion and science are deeply connected through common roots. One could say that they were separated at birth.

At the first stirrings of civilization the shaman of each tribe or village held the secrets of the spiritual world and of the behavior of the physical world, for these were the same thing. Very early on, a rift began to form between what were perceived to be the realms of the immaterial and the material, so that eventually we had priests and scientists. It has never been a happy division. Quantum mechanics offers intriguing possibilities for a reconverging of the lines.

What quantum mechanics tells us about reality makes it impossible to envision the universe, including ourselves and all of science, as we have envisioned it for most of our history. Assumptions that we have taken for granted cannot be taken for granted anymore; what was believed impossible may no longer seem impossible or even improbable.

It is equally important to recognize that while quantum mechanics has called the nature of reality into question, it is open ended; it leaves us with the questions, closing no doors with answers of its own.

Quantum mechanics does not lead, for instance, to a belief

in the soul, or God, but clearly when all material things are composed of the immaterial, when the basic stuff of the universe is not stuff at all but numbers, probabilities, one can no longer say that it is unscientific to speak of a realm of the immaterial. The argument of classical physics—that only the material, the concrete, is real—is now the unscientific contention.

While quantum mechanics does not posit a soul, or a God, or ghosts, it unquestionably makes new room for them. It makes room, in fact, for the concept of all existence as a thought of God, or even as the mind of God, something set forth some years ago by Howard Nemerov in a poem entitled "Moment," in which

> the mind of God,
> The flash across the gap of being, thinks
> In the instant absence of forever: now.

Do we know nothing, then? We know that we exist, because we can ask the question. We know that we hunger for order. These bind us together and make us one. Beyond these, we are bound together by the very uncertainty we share. And perhaps we can say that because of the universal nature of our hunger, we cannot be yearning for a fiction, so that finally such a hunger will not have been in vain.

So, then, what have we come to? Are there no distinctions to make? Well, that depends, finally, upon whom we are going to distinguish between. If by distinctions we mean to set up a spiritual hierarchy, to establish that the poet is closer to God than the biologist, who is closer to God than the physicist, and on down the line in a kind of Platonic scale of reality—if this is what one means by distinctions, then plainly I refuse to make them.

There are distinctions, certainly. Between people. Not as a declining scale on which each profession is assigned a value but simply as a plumber is not a medical doctor. First there is the empirical distinction. But can we not say that one person's work is—what word do you want to use?—truer, more real, better than another's? The answer is yes, of course, but not according to the work. It is according to the motive. It may as easily as not be the doctor who should wash the feet of the plumber.

The physician and the plumber who are both simply looking for a fast buck—and both can get it—are a couple of people working with pipes. The only difference is in the stuff the pipes are made of.

But looking to the subject at hand, there is a second distinction between people. And like the first, it cuts across vocational lines. Almost everyone, as I have noted, looks for order or wants to create it. The distinction is in *this:* There are those who want to draw order out of confusion, and there are those who want to impose order *on* confusion. The second is destined to failure, sooner or later, because when one imposes order on confusion, what order there is rests on chaos as a base. To serve the human spirit, order must be a thing crystallized out of the solution we call nature.

You may remember a chemistry class in which a supersaturated solution in a test tube seemed a perfectly clear liquid, without form and void. But suddenly, when the temperature was lowered a degree or the test tube was tapped, a marvelous crystalline structure formed within it. You could have poured the solution into a honeycomb structure and given it a pattern, but it would not have been the inherent pattern, nor one that would stay if the honeycomb fell away. Hitler tried to turn the Polish people into Germans. Some parents expect all their children to conform to a master concept of order, not realizing that within every child is a natural and proper sense of order to be drawn out. It is even true of every classroom. Of every marriage.

The scientist and the humanist, the engineer and the philosopher, the artist and the politician all may work to bring out of the nature of things the order that is within. Conversely, they may all attempt to impose on thing *as they are* things *as they would have them.*

So we have bridges that stay and bridges that fall, philosophies that guide and philosophies that mislead, poems that come to us as forceful experiences and poems that turn us away, a political order that enriches the human spirit and a political order that dwarfs and twists it.

Of course distinctions fall between us, and they should. But those that are most important, finally, are not those between professions, vocations, pursuits but those between people driven by purposes they would be glad to reveal to their children and people driven by purposes they hide behind sham, behind the easy lie of lip service to larger things.

The distinction that matters most lies here; it falls between those who believe that there is an inherent order in things waiting to be drawn out and those who believe there is no order except what is forced on nature, human or otherwise. Let us have enough men and women who are idealistic enough to pass this test and realistic enough to pass it, and we may have another Renaissance, a flourishing of human culture in all its parts together, as the world has never dreamed of.

Backstreet Affair

The Writer and the Publisher in the Smoky Bars of Small Imprints and No Advances

*I*magine a motel a little too far from town to be of use to business travelers, with frame cabins and a gravel drive. There's a plaster flamingo under a sign where the NO before VACANCY is never lit. Inside one of the rooms are two lovers. On the luggage, the initials NCP and SPA for Non-Commercial Publisher and Serious Press Author. We could as well have taken the letters to mean Noble, Crazy, and Proud for the first and Someone Nearly Anonymous for the other.

We might assume that there is something illegal, if not immoral, going on here, something that will not last until sunrise; in fact, our lovers share a profound commitment, even if the author occasionally has fantasies of an uptown affair and the noncommercial publisher would like to make the thing a triangle that includes the librarian who has never paid him much mind.

Now, the noncommercial publisher may be a small independent press or an academic press; they have in common a concern for quality over cash, a fondness for books as an idea, and a sense of the simple pleasure in publishing them.

The small independent press, though, has never been afforded the respect that normally attaches to an academic press, which, though sometimes thought of as stodgy, is also seen in academic regalia and therefore as somehow important.

To many people, *small independent press* means a foot-treadle roller press in the garage or basement printing chapbooks of poetry and strange short stories by subculture writers not ready for prime time. Publication with a small independent press won't bring a raise or promotion to a young college faculty member. Most bookstores and libraries won't order books published by small independent presses unless the bookstore manager or librarian knows the author personally. We imagine a world of nice elderly ladies and cranky old gentlemen, unreconstructed anarchists and conspiratorial graduate students.

The perception is as wrong as any stereotype, but like every generalization it arose from particulars that were taken too far.

The very names of these presses in many cases have created the same credibility problems we would have with the Guess-What Pharmacy or Bernice's Airline; they often suggest little mansard-roofed boutiques called Things & Stuff, as the studied freshness in the christening of small presses gives way to a new banality, and one is tempted to join in with the Wine Press, the Permanent Press, and the Full-Court Press.

Compounding this, the small independent press is likely to be either artsy, on one hand, or utterly indifferent in matters of design, on the other, and—perhaps because earning a livelihood is a separate burden—is sometimes undependable in correspondence and casual in fiscal matters. To make matters more difficult, the author has been known to act with condescension toward the small press, as one might toward an unattractive partner in a marriage of convenience.

University presses often experience similar condescension, not from their authors, but from the reading public when they publish nonscholarly books. No one questions the value of a monograph on protolinguistics, but an author whose poetry or fiction is published by a university press may be seen as not quite the equal of those who make it in the real world. This is much less the case with poetry than with fiction, since no one makes

money off poetry anyway, and since such poets as Howard Nemerov and John Ciardi published with university presses.

The publication of fiction with a university press, especially
long fiction, is in the minds of many readers simply to throw
it away. Someone asks you who published your book. You tell
them it was Upstate University Press, and the reaction is ". . . oh
. . . I see. . . . That's interesting."

So what are these presses for, besides the publication of high-
toned scholarship and thin volumes of poetry with pages that
have raggedy edges? What good do they do?

Apart from scholarship, vanity, and the need for a hobby,
university and small independent presses did very little until
the early 1960s. Pro bono publishing, the publishing of worthy
works that relatively few people want to read, was once the mark
of the "gentleman publisher," the man who had founded, or
whose family had founded, the firm he ran as his own domain:
Alfred Knopf, Jack Dutton, the Harcourts and the Putnams, and
Bennet Cert at Random House. Then something happened to
change all that.

Shortly after midcentury a frenzy of mergers and takeovers
hit all areas of the business world just as family ties to the old
publishing houses were weakening. The founders' several children and grandchildren, great-nephews and great-nieces, represented a natural dissipation of interest in the family business,
so that such houses as Knopf, Random House, and Dutton were
bought by such firms as Xerox and General Foods, whose boards
were inclined to look upon the books purely as products and
inventory; in consequence, the editors and marketing people at
these houses, traditionally responsible for deciding what to publish, in how many copies, and how long to keep it in print found

themselves joined in the decisions by the firms' accountants. Increasingly, manuscripts came to be judged only in terms of sales potential.

This was always a consideration, of course; the old houses had to survive, and a publisher could not live on red ink, but it was thought a good and proper thing for some works of value to be made available if they made only a little money, and some perhaps if they only broke even. We have reached the point now at which the expense of warehousing taxable inventory forces the pulping of great numbers of titles whose sales fall below a level established by a firm's business office.

It would be unfair to denigrate companies with no tradition in publishing for going the way they have always gone as successful enterprises and making as much money for their shareholders as possible, but the fact is that it means the assurance of mass appeal in every title published, which in turn means, with few exceptions, the genre novel (mystery, romance, horror, science fiction, spy, western), written for the most part by blockbuster names, and then self-help books, how-to books, comic-strip reprints, and exposés. Only a few well-established serious novelists have followings large enough to keep them on board.

This means that except for the biggest and proven names (and the occasional newcomer who seems a likely replacement for an aging star), collections of poetry, short stories, essays, and the so-called midlist novel (the novel as art; think of Flannery O'Connor, John Williams, Richard Yates, and Carson McCullers) have almost nowhere to go now among the major New York houses, and those that manage to be published there usually find their books in print for a very short time.

The role of the noncommercial publisher changed abruptly

and drastically as both university and small independent presses moved to take up the slack. The small independent presses began to receive more and better manuscripts. University presses expanded their traditional mission to include the publication not only of scholarly works but of any work representing a contribution to its field and likely not to interest the major houses.

To underscore the importance of the noncommercial publisher, here is a picture of what sometimes occurs in the acquisition and marketing of a book by a major house.

First, the house approaches a major bookstore chain with a manuscript, asking the chain for a promise to "front shelf" it for a certain length of time if it's published. After it's published and presented to the publisher's traveling bookstore sales representatives at the appropriate annual sales meeting, the reps scatter to all points with this book and twenty-five or thirty other new titles in hand. Bookstore by bookstore they find, as they knew they would, time to talk only about three or four new books while the store manager breaks for coffee or waits to be taken off hold on the telephone. The rep is obliged to narrow the presentation to three or four or five probable hits, books as similar as possible to those that have been hits before or books the marketing people seemed most excited about at the sales meeting. The orders garnered on these calls flow back into the publisher's marketing department as an obvious trend, confirming the publisher's judgment in the past and the marketing department's intuitive recognition of a bestseller. The publisher shifts its advertising budget to bet on the fast horses. Sales on these few books continue to soar as success fuels success, and any representative who was not at first concentrating the sales pitch on these titles quickly makes the adjustment.

Sales of the books that were not similar to the bestsellers of the past or failed to catch fire in the imaginations of the marketing staff are spoken of less and less—why throw good money after bad?—and therefore sell less and less. An author may be informed in as few as twelve to eighteen months that the balance of the books in the warehouse are to be pulped unless the author wants to buy them, or they may be "remaindered" to a company that buys such inventory at as low as five cents on the dollar, with no royalty on the sale going to the author.

Books perhaps five to ten years in the writing are gone, with little or no chance of being reborn under the imprint of another publisher. I do not think it is overdramatizing to say that this is worse than an unfortunate situation. The right to freedom of speech depends upon the right to a platform; when the complex, the specialized, the unsettling, or the unpopular cannot be published—not just printed but made public—First Amendment rights are called into question.

This is not to say that commercial houses ought to change their ways; it is meaningless to say that what is impossible should happen. It is only to underscore the importance of alternatives to those houses.

Still, the problem does not lend itself to an easy solution. The University of Arkansas, publishing fewer than thirty titles a year when I was its director, was being offered annually upward of four thousand titles, while every year another university press was dropping poetry or fiction from its list, as were one or two of the commercial houses still publishing poetry or serious fiction.

It is true now, whatever else is said, that noncommercial publishers in America do more to promulgate significant literature than any major commercial house. Only New Directions, which has always been small in spirit, has a right to dispute this;

Athenaeum, which closed down shortly after it dropped poetry from its list, might have disputed it.

What can be said today that could not have been imagined in the sixties or even much into the eighties is that some of the best and most important writers of our time have been published outside the pale of the moneyed imprint—Barbara Howes, Anthony Hecht, Ronald Koertge, John Clellon Holmes, Richard Wilbur, William Stafford, Enid Shomer, William Dickey, John Ciardi, Peter Viereck, Howard Nemerov, and Ellen Gilchrist, to name a few. Some excellent writers have been published *only* by noncommercial presses. I think of William Kloefkorn, David Baker, C. D. Wright, Charles Bukowski, and Frank Stanford. And Ardis Press, of Ann Arbor, became the American publisher of Anna Akhmatova.

Everyone makes mistakes. When major publishing houses make them, the effect on the American literary scene can be considerable. There is a chance now for these mistakes to be corrected. The University of Arkansas Press published the short stories of Frederic Raphael, Tom T. Hall, and Ellen Gilchrist after they had crossed the desks of most of the acquisitions editors in New York. The Louisiana State University Press published John Kennedy Toole's *Confederacy of Dunces* when the stack of rejection slips was beginning to look like the manuscript itself.

But it's not enough to buy from a few small presses the few books bearing distinguished names. To buy only those books from noncommercial presses written by well-known writers is to go to Rome and stay at the Holiday Inn. What's most valuable and exciting about small presses is the possibility of discovery. So here they are, not quite slipping around but not always invited to the best parties either. The day may come when our two lovers will have a respectable union and go to well-lit places, but I'm not certain we ought to hope for it too ardently. An affair sometimes loses its magic when it leaves the backstreets.

Maybe we ought not become too respectable.

What Stone Walls Make

$\mathcal{O}$ne Saturday morning a guard in an Arkansas prison bumped an inmate awake with orders to get up and get out on a work detail. The inmate focused an eye and said he was supposed to go to class that morning.

"You're going to work," the guard said, and tapped the clipboard in his hand. "Name's on the list: pottery workshop."

An hour later the inmate and twenty others marched single-file to the workshop, where for three hours they paid close attention to the making of poetry. Not pottery. The well-wrought urn. We laughed about it.

This was the third of three workshops funded by a grant to the Arkansas Arts Council from the National Endowment for the Arts. The small grant took me to five units of the state correctional system each week: three Saturday visits, for the men's and women's units at Cummins Penitentiary and for Tucker Intermediate Penitentiary (for younger men convicted of heavy crimes), then two Sunday visits, for the boys' and girls' reformatories at Wrightsville and Alexander. The five institutions are located within a radius of thirty miles from Pine Bluff. Still it was a lot of driving—I live more than two hundred miles from Cummins—and a lot of workshop for one weekend. But baseball players know the meaning of sacrifice. What comes back on the investment—though not much of one, at that—is too large and too formless, maybe, to get words around, but I went to the prisons as long and as often as I could get money for the round-trips. I am not, as Byron said after an experience that turned him around, what I was before.

This was the last session we had funds for, and the inmates were as concerned as I was that the workshops would stop. It was important for a lot of reasons that they go on.

It was important partly because some of the men and women were writing well enough to publish, and might, if they didn't lose the drive and a chance for criticism along the way, turn out some good and serious work. It was important—and this matters more—because the members of the workshops were learning to use words and be at ease with them.

The common denominators of the prison population are fear, frustration, loneliness, and anger. The anger is not directed at the police or the guards or even the laws so much as at the men and women who represent the erratic administration of justice. They know that on another day or in another county the sentence might have been six years or twelve months or even suspended instead of twelve or fifteen years. They are angry about that. And at themselves.

The failures of the judicial system, where money and color and position sometimes matter as much as they do at the country club, and of the penal system, where rehabilitation is sometimes given about as much attention as it is at the country club, are known well enough. Nothing I say here is going to change it. Nothing said in a poem is going to change it either. But some of the inmates found that one way to control the fear and the loneliness, the frustration and the anger, was to write about those abiding facts of their lives, to use them as fuel to make their poems move. And they found that the fuel burned better if the poems were well made.

And they came to realize, some of them, that if they had been able to command the language they were born to and on which virtually all effective communication depends, they might not have been where they were. Those raised with words have trouble realizing the radical (let that word go to its root) implication of this. Not counting embezzlers and students in for drug-law violations, the great difference is verbal.

Well, after that workshop, when we'd said tentative good-byes that none of us quite believed, I hunted around the state until I discovered a foundation that makes educational grants. They let us have enough for three more visits. That is, to the men's and women's units at Cummins. It wasn't a large grant; a choice had to be made. There were schools at the boys' and girls' reformatories, where someone did talk about poems, and there was a school for the young men at Tucker.

At Cummins there's no time for language to move through patterns except in the poetry workshops. So I stayed there, going every other week, to spread it out, collecting more poems for each session than could possibly be covered, listening to the inmates' own criticisms—more and more to the point and tough—of the poems we'd printed up and passed out, and hearing one or another suggest that his or her poem be skipped over, flaws not seen at first having risen embarrassingly to the surface.

I learned as they learned. What *grue* is, and Class III, P.E. Date, and flat time. Mostly, though, I learned about poetry and about myself. About human beings, myself being one on good days. We learned.

There are moments that stay luminous:

Jordan, my wife, and I were walking across the grounds with some of the poets at the women's unit when one of the women who didn't ever talk said it was important that we came;

A girl at Alexander said she'd decided to work when she got

out to earn money and to go on to school because she'd discovered that her earlier teachers had been more afraid of poetry than she was;

A black man with a quiet voice finally took off his shades after five sessions, fifteen hours, grinned once, and then laughed out loud when I said he'd broken every rule of the game in a single poem—and that it was a good poem, the best he'd written;

An inmate at the tail end of the line who'd heard it somewhere, said, "Happy Birthday" to me as he followed the others through the barred door where I turned them over to the guards after each workshop;

A nineteen-year-old inmate who'd set his poems to music sang us those country blues until we almost forgot where we were.

KUAF, the FM station of the University of Arkansas, dedicated a program to poems from the prison workshops—closing with good songs—without any of the disclaimer the producer of the show expected to have to make. Any worksheet from the prisons is better reading than most college literary magazines and better than some work in the established journals. This is maybe because the inmates are mostly coachable and serious about writing well. Maybe it's because they've looked back of their eyeballs. They know that most human statements contain their own contradictions and that most human acts contain the seeds of their own defeat. They understand that every person is a battlefield. They understand survival.

I was using them for something, and they knew it. They were using me, and I knew it. This is the nature of the human compact. This is the selfishness of a larger self, and we knew it.